(oh) (ahl-fah-beh-too)
O Alfabeto
the   alphabet

Throughout this book you will find an easy pronunciation guide above all new words. Refer to this Step whenever you need help, but remember, spend no longer than *10 minutes a day*®.

Many letters in Portuguese are pronounced just as they are in English, at least part of the time!

(b)	(d)	(f)	(g)	(l)	(m)	(n)	(p)	(r)	(s)	(t)	(v)	(x)	(z)
b	d	f	g	l	m	n	p	r	s	t	v	x	z

Here is a guide to help you learn the sounds of the Portuguese letters which are pronounced somewhat differently. Practice these sounds with the examples given which are mostly first names.

Portuguese letter	English sound	Examples	Write it here
a	ah	**A**n**a** *(ah-nah)*	
ai	eye / i / y	**Jai**me *(zhy-mee)*	
au	ow *(as in how)*	**Pau**lo *(pow-loo)*	
c *(before e and i)*	s	Ali**c**e *(ah-lee-see)*	
c *(before a, o, u)*	k	**C**atarina *(kah-tah-ree-nah)*	Catarina, Catarina
ç	s	Igua**ç**u *(ee-gwah-soo)* waterfall on Brazilian-Argentinian border	
ch	sh *(as in jeep)*	**Ch**uí *(shoo-ee)* town on Brazilian-Uruguayan border	
d *(before e and i)*	j	**D**iana *(jee-ah-nah)*	
e	eh *(as in let)*	**E**l**e**na *(eh-leh-nah)*	
e *(at word end)*	ee	Simon**e** *(see-moh-nee)*	
ei	ay *(as in day)*	R**ei**naldo *(hay-nahl-doo)*	
er	air	**Fer**nando *(fair-nahn-doo)*	
eu	eh-oo	**Eu**gênio *(eh-oo-zheh-nee-oo)*	
g *(before e and i)*	zh	**G**ina *(zhee-nah)*	
h	silent	**H**aroldo *(ah-rohl-doo)*	
i	ee	C**í**n**ti**a *(seen-chee-ah)*	
j	zh	**J**osé *(zhoh-zeh)*	
lh	l-y	i**lh**a *(eel-yah)* island	

3

Letter	Sound	Example	Write it here
nh	*(as in canyon)* n-y	**se<u>nh</u>or** *(sehn-yor)* Mr.	_____
o	oh oo	**<u>O</u>rland<u>o</u>** *(or-lahn-doo)*	_____
oi	oy	**<u>oi</u>!** *(oy)* hi	_____
ou	oh	**<u>Ou</u>ro Preto** *(oh-roo)(preh-too)* town, World Cultural Heritage Site	_____
(before e and i) **qu**	k	**par<u>qu</u>e** *(par-kay)* park	_____
(before a and o) **qu**	kw	**<u>qu</u>atro** *(kwah-troo)* four	_____
(initially) **r**	h	**<u>R</u>osana** *(hoh-zah-nah)*	Rosana, Rosana
rr	r-h	**te<u>rr</u>a** *(tair-hah)* land	_____
(between vowels) **s**	z	**I<u>s</u>abel** *(ee-zah-bel)*	_____
(at word end) **s**	s / sh	**Carlo<u>s</u>** *(kar-loosh)*	_____
(before e and i) **t**	ch	**Vicen<u>t</u>e** *(vee-sehn-chee)*	_____
u	oo	**Úrs<u>u</u>la** *(oor-soo-lah)*	_____
(initially and after ai, e, ei, ou, n) **x**	sh	**Ale<u>x</u>andre** *(ah-leh-shahn-dree)*	_____
(at syllable end) **z**	s / sh	**Beatri<u>z</u>** *(beh-ah-trees)*	_____

Note: In addition to the sounds above, Portuguese has many nasal sounds. Whenever you see a tilde (˜) over a vowel, think nasal!

ã	ahn	**irm<u>ã</u>** *(eer-mahn)* sister	_____
	("ow" as in how plus "n")	**amanh<u>ã</u>** *(ah-mahn-yahn)* tomorrow	_____
ão	own	**Jo<u>ão</u>** *(zhoh-own)*	_____
		S<u>ão</u> Paulo *(sown)(pow-loo)*	_____
õe	oyn	**cart<u>õe</u>s** *(kar-toynsh)* cards	_____
		dir<u>e</u>ções *(jee-reh-soynsh)* directions	_____

If you were able to pronounce **direções** without hesitating, give yourself a giant pat on the back!

Accents such as ^ (**ê**) and ´ (**é**) are used to indicate stress, either in the word or even in a sentence. See **Cíntia, Úrsula, Eugênio,** and **José** above.

Sometimes the phonetics may seem to contradict your pronunciation guide. Don't panic! The easiest and best possible phonetics have been chosen for each individual word. Pronounce the phonetics just as you see them. Don't over-analyze them. Speak with a Portuguese accent and, above all, enjoy yourself!

PORTUGUESE

in 10 minutes a day®

by Kristine K. Kershul, M.A., University of California, Santa Barbara

Consultant: Rosana do Rio Broom

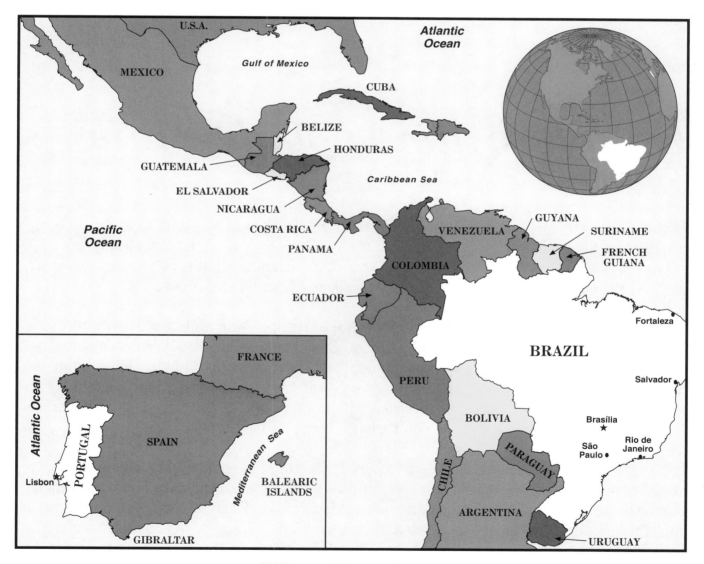

Bilingual Books, Inc.

1719 West Nickerson Street, Seattle, WA 98119
Tel: (206) 284-4211 Fax: (206) 284-3660
www.10minutesaday.com • www.bbks.com

ISBN: 978-1-931873-33-8

Fourth edition. Second printing, July 2017.

Can you say this?

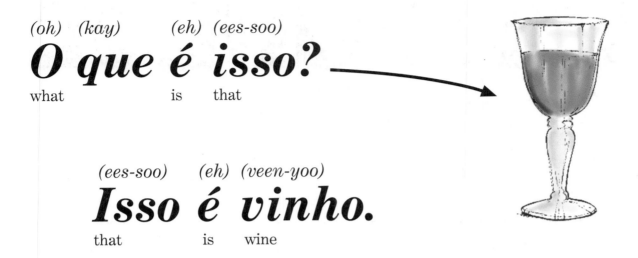

(oh) *(kay)* *(eh)* *(ees-soo)*
O que é isso?
what   is   that

(ees-soo) *(eh)* *(veen-yoo)*
Isso é vinho.
   that   is   wine

(eh-oo) *(kair-oo)* *(oom)* *(koh-poo)* *(jee)* *(veen-yoo)*
Eu quero um copo de vinho.
I   want   a   glass   of   wine

If you can say this, you can learn to speak Portuguese. You will be able to easily order wine, lunch, theater tickets, pastry, or anything else you wish. You simply ask **"O que é isso?"** *(oh) (kay) (eh) (ees-soo)* and, upon learning what it is, you can order it with **"Eu quero isso"** *(eh-oo) (kair-oo) (ees-soo)*. Sounds easy, doesn't it?

The purpose of this book is to give you an **immediate** speaking ability in Portuguese. Portuguese is spoken not only in Portugal and Brazil, but in Angola, Mozambique and other countries as well. Using the acclaimed *"10 minutes a day®"* methodology, you will aquire a large working vocabulary that will suit your needs, and you will acquire it almost automatically. To aid you, this book offers a unique and easy system of pronunciation above each word which walks you through learning Portuguese.

If you are planning a trip or moving to where Portuguese is spoken, you will be leaps ahead of everyone if you take just a few minutes a day to learn the easy key words that this book offers. Start with Step 1 and don't skip around. Each day work as far as you can comfortably go in those 10 minutes. Don't overdo it. Some days you might want to just review. If you forget a word, you can always look it up in the glossary. Spend your first 10 minutes studying the map on the previous page. And yes, have fun learning your new language.

As you work through the Steps, always use the special features which only this series offers. You have sticky labels and flash cards, free words, puzzles, and quizzes. When you have completed the book, cut out the menu guide and take it along on your trip.

When you arrive in **Brasil,** *(brah-zeel)* **Portugal** *(por-too-gahl)* or another Portuguese-speaking country, the very first thing you will need to do is ask questions — "Where **(onde)** *(ohn-jee)* is the bus stop?" "**Onde** *(ohn-jee)* where can I exchange money?" "**Onde** *(ohn-jee)* where is the lavatory?" "**Onde** *(ohn-jee)* where is a restaurant?" "**Onde** *(ohn-jee)* where do I catch a taxi?" "**Onde** is a good hotel?" "**Onde** is my luggage?" — and the list will go on and on for the entire length of your visit. In Portuguese, there are SEVEN KEY QUESTION WORDS to learn. For example, the seven key question words will help you find out exactly what you are ordering in a restaurant before you order it — and not after the surprise (or shock!) arrives. Notice that only one letter is different in the Portuguese words for "when" and "how much." Don't confuse them! Take a few minutes to practice saying the seven key question words listed below. Then cover the Portuguese with your hand and fill in each of the blanks with the matching Portuguese **palavra.** *(pah-lah-vrah)* word

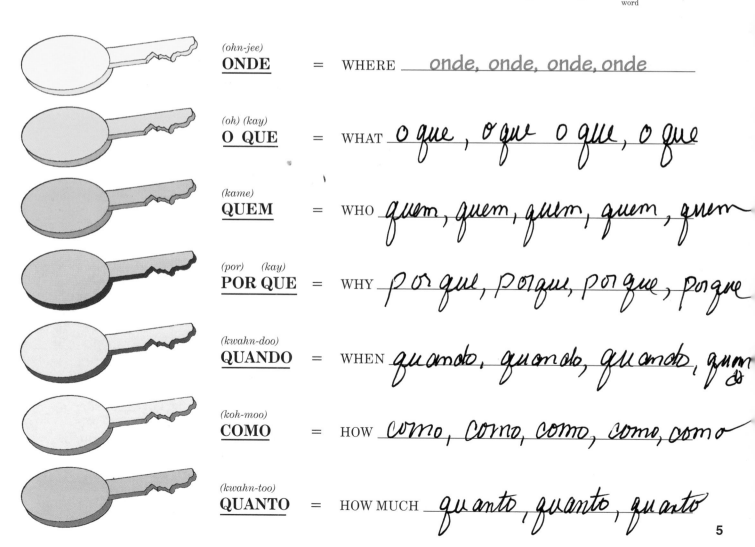

(ohn-jee)
ONDE = WHERE _onde, onde, onde, onde_

(oh) (kay)
O QUE = WHAT _O que, o que o que, o que_

(kame)
QUEM = WHO _quem, quem, quem, quem, quem_

(por) (kay)
POR QUE = WHY _por que, porque, por que, porque_

(kwahn-doo)
QUANDO = WHEN _quando, quando, quando, quando_

(koh-moo)
COMO = HOW _como, como, como, como, como_

(kwahn-too)
QUANTO = HOW MUCH _quanto, quanto, quanto_

Now test yourself to see if you really can keep these **palavras** *(pah-lah-vrahs)* **words** straight in your mind. Draw lines

between the Portuguese **e** *(eh)* **and** English equivalents below.

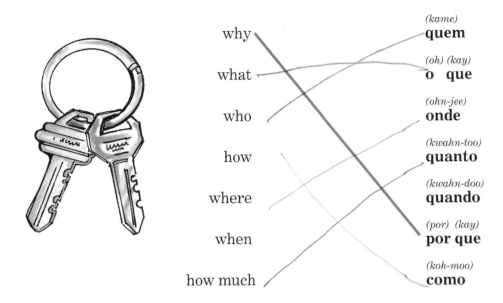

why	**quem** *(kame)*
what	**o que** *(oh) (kay)*
who	**onde** *(ohn-jee)*
how	**quanto** *(kwahn-too)*
where	**quando** *(kwahn-doo)*
when	**por que** *(por) (kay)*
how much	**como** *(koh-moo)*

Examine the following questions containing these **palavras** *(pah-lah-vrahs)*. Practice the sentences out loud **e** *(eh)* **and**

then practice by copying the Portuguese in the blanks underneath each question.

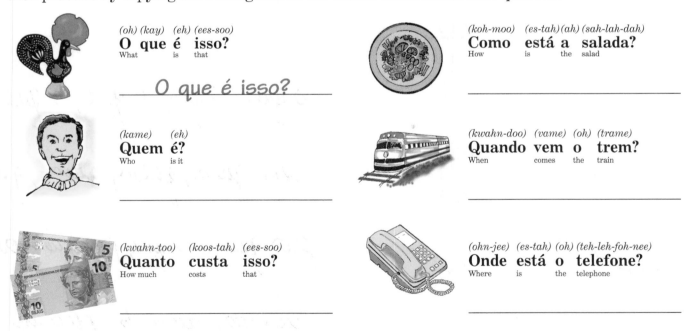

O que é isso? *(oh) (kay) (eh) (ees-soo)*
What   is   that

O que é isso?

Quem é? *(kame) (eh)*
Who   is it

_____

Quanto custa isso? *(kwahn-too) (koos-tah) (ees-soo)*
How much   costs   that

_____

Como está a salada? *(koh-moo) (es-tah) (ah) (sah-lah-dah)*
How   is   the   salad

_____

Quando vem o trem? *(kwahn-doo) (vame) (oh) (trame)*
When   comes   the   train

_____

Onde está o telefone? *(ohn-jee) (es-tah) (oh) (teh-leh-foh-nee)*
Where   is   the   telephone

_____

"Onde" *(ohn-jee)* will be your most used question **palavra**. *(pah-lah-vrah)* Say each of the following Portuguese

sentences aloud. Then write out each sentence without looking at the example. If you don't

succeed on the first try, don't give up. Just practice each sentence until you are able to do it

easily. Remember **"ei"** is pronounced like "ay" in "day" **e** *(eh)* **and** **"ai"** is pronounced "eye."

(ohn-jee) (eh) (oh) (bahn-yay-roo)
Onde é o banheiro?
Where is the restroom

DAMAS CAVALHEIROS

(es-tah) (oh) (tahk-see)
Onde está o táxi?
Where is the taxi

(oh) (ow-nee-boos)
Onde está o ônibus?
Where is the bus

_____   *Onde está o táxi?*   _____

(eh) (oh) (hehs-tow-rahn-chee)
Onde é o restaurante?
is restaurant

(bahn-koo)
Onde é o banco?
is bank

(oh-tel)
Onde é o hotel?
hotel

_____   _____   _____

(seem)
Sim, you can see similarities between **inglês** *(een-glaysh)* and **português** *(por-too-gaysh)* if you look closely. You will be
yes   English   Portuguese

amazed at the number of **palavras** *(pah-lah-vrahs)* which are identical (or almost identical) in both languages.
words

Of course, they do not always sound the same when spoken by a Portuguese-speaker, but

the similarities will certainly surprise you **e** *(eh)* make your work here easier. Listed below are five

"free" **palavras** beginning with " **a** " *(ah)* to help you get started. Be sure to say each **palavra** aloud

e *(eh)* then write out the Portuguese **palavra** in the blank to the right. Remember whenever you see

"ow" in the phonetics, it is like the "ow" in "how" or "cow."

☑ **abril** *(ah-breel)* . . . . April		_abril, abril, abril, abril, abril_
❑ **absoluto** *(ahb-soh-loo-too)* . . . . absolute		_____
❑ **absurdo** *(ahb-soor-doo)* . . . . absurd	**a**	_____
❑ **o acidente** *(ah-see-dehn-chee)* . . . . accident		_____
❑ **agosto** *(ah-gohs-too)* . . . . August		_____

Free **palavras** like these will appear at the bottom of the following pages in a yellow color band.

They are easy — enjoy them! Remember, in Portuguese, the letter **"h"** **é** *(eh)* silent.
is

7

(por-too-gaysh)
Português has multiple **palavras** for "the" and "a," but they are very easy. If the Portuguese
Portuguese   words

word ends in "**a**" (feminine) it *usually* will have the article "**a**" or "**uma**." If the word ends in
                                                                    (ah)   *(oo-mah)*
                                                                    the   a

"**o**" (masculine) it *usually* will have the article "**o**" or "**um**." Of course there are exceptions!
                                                       (oh)   *(oom)*
                                                       the   a

(oh) (meh-nee-noo)
o menino
the boy

(ohs) (meh-nee-noosh)
os meninos
the boys

(ah) (meh-nee-nah)
a menina
the girl

(ahs) (meh-nee-nahs)
as meninas
the girls

(trame)
o trem
the train

(trains)
os trens
the trains

(oo-mah) (pah-lah-vrah)
uma palavra
a   word

(oo-mahs) (pah-lah-vrahs)
umas palavras
some   words

(oo-mah) (ah-meh-ree-kah-nah)
uma americana
an   American (female)

(oo-mahs) (ah-meh-ree-kah-nahs)
umas americanas
some   Americans (female)

(oom) (ah-meh-ree-kah-noo)
um americano
an   American (male)

(oons) (ah-meh-ree-kah-noosh)
uns americanos
some   Americans (male or mixed)

(een-glaysh)
At first this might appear difficult, but only because it is different from **inglês.** Just remember
                                                                             English

you will be understood whether you say "**a palavra**" or "**o palavra**." Soon you will automatically

select the right article without even thinking about it.

In Step 2 you were introduced to the Seven Key
QuestionWords. These seven words are the basics, the
most essential building blocks for learning Portuguese.
Throughout this book you will come across keys
asking you to fill in the missing question word. Use
this opportunity not only to fill in the blank on that
key, but to review all your question words. Play with
the new sounds, speak slowly and have fun.

❑ **a agricultura** *(ah-gree-kool-too-rah)*	agriculture	_____
❑ **a álgebra** *(ahl-zhee-brah)*	algebra	_____
❑ **a América** *(ah-meh-ree-kah)*	America	_____
❑ **o animal** *(ah-nee-mahl)*	animal	_____
❑ **anual** *(ah-noo-ahl)*	annual	_____

a

Before you proceed with this Step, situate yourself comfortably in your living room. Now look
around you. Can you name the things that you see in this **sala** *(sah-lah)* in Portuguese? You can probably
guess **o telefone** *(teh-leh-foh-nee)* and maybe even **o sofá.** *(soh-fah)* Let's learn the rest of them. After practicing these
palavras out loud, write them in the blanks below.

(oh) (ah-bah-zhoor)
o abajur _AFAJUR_
the   lamp

(soh-fah)
o sofá _SOFA_
sofa

(ah) (kah-day-rah)
a cadeira _CADEIRA_
the   chair

(tah-peh-chee)
o tapete _TAPETE_
carpet

(ah) (meh-zah)
a mesa _a mesa, a mesa_
the   table

(por-tah)
a porta _PORTA_
door

(heh-loh-zhee-oo)
o relógio _RELÓGIO_
clock / watch

(kor-chee-nah)
a cortina _CORTINA_
curtain

(teh-leh-foh-nee)
o telefone _TELEFONE_
telephone

(ah) (zhah-neh-lah)
a janela
the   window

(kwah-droo)
o quadro
picture

You will notice that the correct form of <u>o</u> or <u>a</u> is given **com** *(kohm)* each noun. This tells you whether the
noun is masculine (**o**) or feminine (**a**). Now open your **livro** *(lee-vroo)* to the sticky labels on page 17 and
later on page 35. Peel off the first 11 labels **e** *(eh)* proceed around **a sala,** *(sah-lah)* labeling these items in
your home. This will help to increase your Portuguese **palavra** power easily. Don't forget to say
each **palavra** as you attach the label.

Now ask yourself, **"Onde está o abajur?"** *(ohn-jee)* *(ah-bah-zhoor)* **e** point at it while you answer, **"O abajur** *(ah-bah-zhoor)* **está**
is   *lamp*   *is*
ali." *(ah-lee)* Continue on down the list above until you feel comfortable with these new **palavras.**
there

❑ **a aplicação** *(ah-plee-kah-sown)*	application	_____
❑ **a/o artista** *(ar-chees-tah)*	artist	_____
❑ **a atenção** *(ah-tehn-sown)*	attention **a**	_____
❑ **ativo** *(ah-chee-voo)*	active	_____
❑ **o ato** *(ah-too)*	act (of a play)	

(kah-zah)
a casa = the house

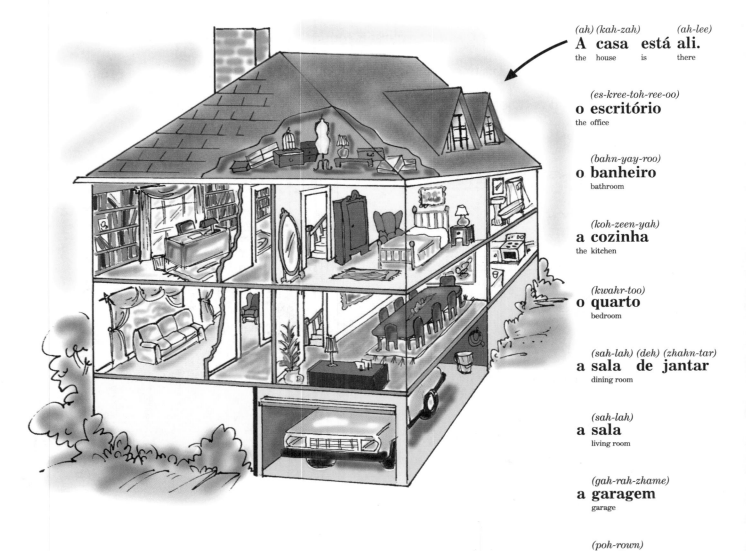

(ah) (kah-zah) *(ah-lee)*
A casa está ali.
the house is there

(es-kree-toh-ree-oo)
o escritório
the office

(bahn-yay-roo)
o banheiro
bathroom

(koh-zeen-yah)
a cozinha
the kitchen

(kwahr-too)
o quarto
bedroom

(sah-lah) (deh) (zhahn-tar)
a sala de jantar
dining room

(sah-lah)
a sala
living room

(gah-rah-zhame)
a garagem
garage

(poh-rown)
o porão
basement

While learning these new **palavras,** let's not forget:

(oh) (kar-hoo)
o carro
the car

CARRO NÃO CARO

(ah) (moh-toh-see-kleh-tah)
a motocicleta
the motorcycle

MOTOCICLETA

(bee-see-kleh-tah)
a bicicleta
bicycle

BICICLETA

☐ **o balão** *(bah-lown)*	balloon	
☐ **o balcão** *(bahl-kown)*	balcony	
☐ **o banco** *(bahn-koo)*	bank	**b**
☐ **básico** *(bah-zee-koo)*	basic	
☐ **o bife** *(bee-fee)*	beefsteak	

(gah-too)
o gato
cat

(zhar-deem)
o jardim
garden

(ahs) (floh-reesh)
as flores
flowers

~~ᴄᴏᴛᴀ~~

o jardim, o jardim

FLORES

(kah-shor-hoo) *(kown)*
o cachorro / o cão
dog   dog

CÃO

(ah) (ky-shah) (doh) (kor-hay-oo)
a caixa do correio
mailbox

caixa do correio

CAIXA DE CORREIO

(ah) (kor-hehs-pohn-dane-see-ah)
a correspondência
mail

CORRESPONDÊNCIA

Peel off the next set of labels **e** wander through your **casa** *(kah-sah)* learning these new **palavras**. It will be somewhat difficult to label **o gato,** *(gah-too)* **as flores** *(floh-reesh)* **ou o** *(oh)* **cachorro,** *(kah-shor-hoo)* but be creative. Practice by asking yourself, **"Onde está o carro?"** *(kar-hoo)* and reply, **"O carro está ali."** *(ah-lee)*
cat   flowers   or   dog
car   there

Onde está a casa?
is

❏ **a calma** *(kahl-mah)* .... calm		_____
❏ **a capacidade** *(kah-pah-see-dah-jee)* .... capacity		_____
❏ **a capela** *(kah-peh-lah)* .... chapel	**c**	_____
❏ **a capital** *(kah-pee-tahl)* .... capital		_____
❏ **o caramelo** *(kah-rah-meh-loo)* .... caramel		_____

(oom) *(doysh)* *(traysh)*
Um, dois, três!
one   two   three

Consider for a minute how important numbers are. How could you tell someone your phone number, your address *(oh)* **ou** or your hotel room if you had no numbers? And think of how difficult it would be if you could not understand the time, the price of an apple *(oh)* **ou** the correct bus to take. When practicing *(ohs)* **os** *(noo-meh-roosh)* **números** numbers below, notice the similarities which have been underlined for you between *(oy-too)* **oito** eight and *(deh-zoy-too)* **dezoito,** eighteen *(noh-vee)* **nove** nine and *(deh-zeh-noh-vee)* **dezenove,** nineteen and so on.

0	*(zeh-roo)* **zero**	Zero, Zero, Zero	10	*(dehsh)* **dez**	dez, dez
1	*(oom)* **um**	um, um, um	11	*(ohn-zee)* **onze**	onze, once, once
2	*(doysh)* **dois**	dois, dois, dois	12	*(doh-zee)* **doze**	doze, doze, doze
3	*(traysh)* **três**	três, três, três	13	*(treh-zee)* **treze**	treze, treze,
4	*(kwah-troo)* **quatro**	quatro, quatro, quatro	14	*(kwah-tor-zee)* **quatorze** *(kah-tor-zee)* **/catorze**	quatorze, quatroz
5	*(seen-koo)* **cinco**	cinco, cinco, cinco	15	*(keen-zee)* **quinze**	quinze, quinz
6	*(saysh)* **seis**	seis, seis, seis	16	*(deh-zehs-saysh)* **dezesseis**	
7	*(seh-chee)* **sete**	sete, sete, sete, sete	17	*(deh-zehs-seh-chee)* **dezessete**	
8	*(oy-too)* **oito**	oito, oito, oito	18	*(deh-zoy-too)* **dezoito**	
9	*(noh-vee)* **nove**	Nove, Nove, Nove	19	*(deh-zeh-noh-vee)* **dezenove**	
10	*(dehsh)* **dez**	dez, dez, dez	20	*(veen-chee)* **vinte**	

☑	**o carro** *(kar-hoo)*	car	*o carro, o carro, o carro, o carro*
☐	**a causa** *(kow-zah)*	cause	
☐	**o centro** *(sehn-troo)*	center	**c**
☐	**o cheque** *(sheck-ee)*	check	
☐	**o chocolate** *(shoh-koh-lah-chee)*	chocolate	

Use these **números** *(noo-meh-roosh)* numbers on a daily basis. Count to yourself **em** **português** *(ehm) (por-too-gaysh)* in Portuguese when you brush your teeth, exercise **ou** *(oh)* commute to work. Fill in the blanks below according to **os números** *(noo-meh-roosh)* numbers given in parentheses. Now is also a good time to learn these two very important phrases.

(eh-oo) (kair-oo)
eu quero ___EU QUERO_____
I   want

(noys) (kair-eh-moosh)
nós queremos ___NÓS QUEREMOS_____
we   want

(eh-oo) (kair-oo)
Eu quero ___um___ (1)
I   want

(kar-town) (pohs-tahl)
cartão postal.
postcard

(kwahn-toosh)
Quantos? ___um___ (1)
how many

Eu quero ___sete___ (7)

(seh-loosh)
selos.
stamps

Quantos? ___sete___ (7)

Eu quero ___oito___ (8)

(seh-loosh)
selos.
stamps

Quantos? ___oito___ (8)

Eu quero ___cinço___ (5)

selos.

Quantos? ___cinco___ (5)

(noys) (kair-eh-moosh)
Nós queremos ___nove___ (9)
we   want

(kar-toynsh) (pohs-tiesh)
cartões postais.
postcards

Quantos? _____ (9)

Nós queremos ___dez___ (10)
we

(kar-toynsh) (pohs-tiesh)
cartões postais.
postcards

Quantos? _____ (10)

(eh-oo) (kair-oo)
Eu quero ___um___ (1)

(een-grehs-soo)
ingresso.
ticket

Quantos? _____ (1)

(kair-eh-moosh)
Nós queremos ___quatro___ (4)
we

(een-grehs-soos)
ingressos.
tickets

Quantos? _____ (4)

Nós queremos ___onze___ (11)

(een-grehs-soos)
ingressos.

Quantos? _____ (11)

Eu quero ___tres___ (3)

(shee-kah-rahs) (deh) (shah)
xícaras de chá.
cups   of   tea

(kwahn-tahs)
Quantas? _____ (3)

Nós queremos ___quatro___ (4)

(koh-poosh) (jee) (ah-gwah)
copos de água.
glasses of   water

(how many)
_____ (4)

☐	**científico** *(see-ehn-chee-fee-koo)*	scientific	
☐	**o cinema** *(see-neh-mah)*	cinema	
☐	**clássico** *(klahs-see-koo)*	classical, classic	**c**
☐	**o closet** *(kloh-zet)*	closet	
☐	**cômico** *(koh-mee-koo)*	comical	

Now see if you can translate the following thoughts into **português.** The answers are provided
Portuguese

upside down at the bottom of the **página.**
(pah-zhee-nah)
page

1. I want seven postcards.

    _____

2. I want nine stamps.

    _____

3. We want four cups of tea.

    _____

4. We want three tickets.

    _____

Review **os números** 1 through 20. Write out your telephone number, fax number, **e** cellular

number. Then write out a friend's telephone number and a relative's telephone number.

(2 0 6) 2 8 4 — 4 2 1 1

dois zero seis _____

(   ) __ __ __ — __ __ __ __

_____

(   ) __ __ __ — __ __ __ __

_____

(ahs) *(koh-reesh)*
As Cores
colors

(ahs) *(koh-reesh)* *(sown)* *(brah-zeel)* *(nohs)* *(es-tah-doosh)* *(oo-nee-doosh)*
As cores são the same **no Brasil** as they are **nos Estados Unidos** — they just have different
colors   are   in   in the   United States

(noh-meesh) *(vee-oh-leh-tah)*
nomes. You can easily recognize **violeta** as violet and **púrpura** as purple. So when you are
names

(kah-zah)(eh)
invited to someone's **casa e** you want to bring flowers, you will be able to order the color you
house

(koh-reesh) *(ahs)*
want. Let's learn the basic **cores**. Once you've learned **as cores,** quiz yourself. What color are

your shoes? Your eyes? Your hair? Your house? Your car? What is your favorite color?

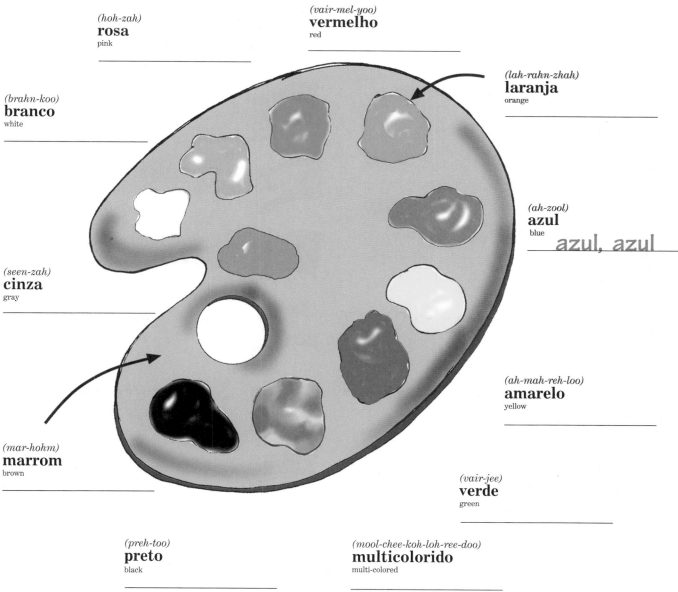

(hoh-zah)
rosa
pink

(vair-mel-yoo)
vermelho
red

(brahn-koo)
branco
white

(lah-rahn-zhah)
laranja
orange

(ah-zool)
azul
blue   azul, azul

(seen-zah)
cinza
gray

(ah-mah-reh-loo)
amarelo
yellow

(mar-hohm)
marrom
brown

(vair-jee)
verde
green

(preh-too)
preto
black

(mool-chee-koh-loh-ree-doo)
multicolorido
multi-colored

❏ **a companhia** *(kohm-pahn-yee-ah)*	company	
❏ **a conversação** *(kohn-vair-sah-sown)*	conversation	
❏ **correto** *(kor-heh-too)*	correct	**c**
❏ **o creme** *(kreh-mee)*......................	cream	
❏ **a cultura** *(kool-too-rah)*..................	culture	

Peel off the next group of labels **e** *(eh)* proceed to label these **cores** *(koh-reesh)* in your **casa.** *(kah-zah)* (house) Identify the two **ou** *(oh)* three dominant colors in the flags below.

azul, branco
Argentina

verde amarelo vermelho
Guinea - Bissau

vermelho, preto
Angola

verde branco amarelo
Mexico

verde amarelo
Brazil

verde amarelo preto
Mozambique

vermelho branco
Canada

verde vermelho
Portugal

azul branco vermelho
Cape Verde Islands

verde vermelho amarelo
São Tomé and Príncipe

vermelho branco azul
Chile

azul verde vermelho
South Africa

amarelo azul vermelho
Colombia

vermelho amarelo
Spain

amarelo azul vermelho
Ecuador

azul branco vermelho
United Kingdom

azul branco vermelho
France

azul branco vermelho
United States

Onde
(where) (where) **está o táxi?** *(oh) (tahk-see)*

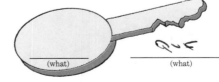
Que
(what) (what) **é isso?** *(eh)(ees-soo)* is that

☐ **a decisão** *(deh-see-sown)* .... decision
☐ **a declaração** *(deh-klah-rah-sown)* .... declaration
☐ **o desconforto** *(dehs-kohn-for-too)* .... discomfort
☐ **a diferença** *(jee-feh-rehn-sah)* .... difference
☐ **a direção** *(jee-reh-sown)* .... direction

d

(ah-bah-zhoor)
o abajur

(kar-hoo)
o carro

(mar-hohm)
marrom

(sair-veh-zhah)
a cerveja

(soh-fah)
o sofá

(moh-toh-see-kleh-tah)
a motocicleta

(vair-mel-yoo)
vermehlo

(lay-chee)
o leite

(kah-day-rah)
a cadeira

(bee-see-kleh-tah)
a bicicleta

(hoh-zah)
rosa

(mahn-tay-gah)
a manteiga

(tah-peh-chee)
o tapete

(gah-too)
o gato

(lah-rahn-zhah)
laranja

(sahl)
o sal

(meh-zah)
a mesa

(zhar-deem)
o jardim

(brahn-koo)
branco

(pee-mehn-tah)
a pimenta

(por-tah)
a porta

(floh-reesh)
as flores

(ah-mah-reh-loo)
amarelo

(koh-poh) *(jee)* *(veen-yoo)*
o copo de vinho

(heh-loh-zhee-oo)
o relógio

(kah-shor-hoo)
o cachorro

(seen-zah)
cinza

(koh-poo)
o copo

(kor-chee-nah)
a cortina

(ky-shah) *(doh)* *(kor-hay-oo)*
a caixa do correio

(preh-too)
preto

(zhor-nahl)
o jornal

(teh-leh-foh-nee)
o telefone

(kor-hehs-pohn-dane-see-ah)
a correspondência

(ah-zool)
azul

(shee-kah-rah)
a xícara

(zhah-neh-lah)
a janela

(zeh-roo)
0 zero

(vair-jee)
verde

(gar-foo)
o garfo

(kwah-droo)
o quadro

(oom)
1 um

(mool-chee-koh-loh-ree-doo)
multicolorido

(fah-kah)
a faca

(kah-zah)
a casa

(doysh)
2 dois

(bohm) *(jee-ah)*
bom dia

(gwahr-dah-nah-poo)
o guardanapo

(es-kree-toh-ree-oo)
o escritório

(traysh)
3 três

(boh-ah) *(tar-jee)*
boa tarde

(prah-too)
o prato

(bahn-yay-roo)
o banheiro

(kwah-troo)
4 quatro

(boh-ah) *(noy-chee)*
boa noite

(kohl-yair)
a colher

(koh-zeen-yah)
a cozinha

(seen-koo)
5 cinco

(oy)
oi

(ar-mah-ree-oo)
o armário

(kwahr-too)
o quarto

(saysh)
6 seis

(chow)
tchau

(shah)
o chá

(sah-lah) *(deh)* *(zhahn-tar)*
a sala de jantar

(seh-chee)
7 sete

(koh-moo) *(vy)*
Como vai?

(kah-fay)
o café

(sah-lah)
a sala

(oy-too)
8 oito

(pown)
o pão

(gah-rah-zhame)
a garagem

(noh-vee)
9 nove

(foh-gown)
o fogão

(por) *(fah-vor)*
por favor

(poh-rown)
o porão

(dehsh)
10 dez

(veen-yoo)
o vinho

(oh-bree-gah-doo)
obrigado

STICKY LABELS

This book has over 150 special sticky labels for you to use as you learn new words. When you are introduced to one of these words, remove the corresponding label from these pages. Be sure to use each of these unique self-adhesive labels by adhering them to a picture, window, lamp, or whatever object it refers to. And yes, they are removable! The sticky labels make learning to speak Portuguese much more fun and a lot easier than you ever expected. For example, when you look in the mirror and see the label, say

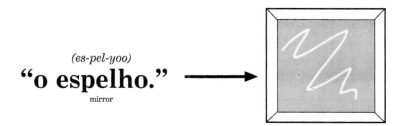

(es-pel-yoo)
"o espelho."
mirror

Don't just say it once, say it again and again. And once you label the refrigerator, you should never again open that door without saying

(zheh-lah-day-rah)
"a geladeira."
refrigerator

By using the sticky labels, you not only learn new words, but friends and family learn along with you! The sooner you start, the sooner you can use these labels at home or work.

(oh) *(jeen-yay-roo)*

O Dinheiro
money

Before starting this Step, go back and review Step 5. It is important that you can count to

(veen-chee)
vinte without looking at **o livro.** Let's learn the larger **números** now. After practicing aloud
twenty   *(lee-vroo)*
book   *(noo-meh-roosh)*

(noo-meh-roosh) *(por-too-gay-zeesh)*
os números **portugueses** 10 through 11,000 below, write these **números** in the blanks provided.
                                                                    (noo-meh-roosh)

Again, notice the similarities between **números** such as **seis** (6), **dezesseis** (16), **sessenta** (60),
                                      (saysh)   *(deh-zehs-saysh)*   *(sehs-sehn-tah)*

(eh) *(saysh)* *(meel)*
e seis mil (6,000).

10	*(dehsh)* **dez** _____		1.000	*(meel)* **mil** _____
20	*(veen-chee)* **vinte** _____		2.000	*(doysh) (meel)* **dois mil** _____
30	*(treen-tah)* **trinta** _____		3.000	*(traysh)* **três mil** _____
40	*(kwah-rehn-tah)* **quarenta** quarenta, quarenta		4.000	*(kwah-troo)* **quatro mil** _____
50	*(seen-kwehn-tah)* **cinqüenta** _____		5.000	*(seen-koo)* **cinco mil** _____
60	*(sehs-sehn-tah)* **sessenta** _____		6.000	*(saysh)* **seis mil** _____
70	*(seh-tehn-tah)* **setenta** _____		7.000	*(seh-chee)* **sete mil** _____
80	*(oy-tehn-tah)* **oitenta** _____		8.000	*(oy-too)* **oito mil** _____
90	*(noh-vehn-tah)* **noventa** _____		9.000	*(noh-vee)* **nove mil** _____
100	*(same)* **cem** _____		10.000	*(dehsh)* **dez mil** _____
500	*(keen-yehn-toosh)* **quinhentos** _____		10.500	*(eh) (keen-yehn-toosh)* **dez mil e quinhentos** _____
1.000	*(meel)* **mil** _____		11.000	*(ohn-zee)* **onze mil** _____

(ah-key) *(doo-ahs)*
Aqui are **duas** important phrases to go with all these **números.** Say them out loud over and
here   two

over and then write them out twice as many times.

(eh-oo) (tehn-yoo)
eu tenho _____
I   have

(noys) (teh-moosh)
nós temos _____
we   have

❏	**discreto** *(jees-kreh-too)*	discreet	_____
❏	**a distância** *(jees-tahn-see-ah)*	distance	_____
❏	**a divisão** *(jee-vee-sown)*	division	**d** _____
❏	**o documento** *(doh-koo-mehn-too)*	document	_____
❏	**o doutor** *(doh-tor)*	doctor (title)	_____

The unit of currency **no Brasil é o real,** *(brah-zeel)* *(eh)* *(heh-ahl)* abbreviated **"R$."** Let's learn the various kinds of
in *is*

moedas e notas. *(moh-eh-dahs)* *(noh-tahs)* Always be sure to practice each **palavra** out loud. You might want to exchange
coins *bills*

some money **agora** *(ah-goh-rah)* so that you can familiarize yourself **com as várias notas e moedas.** *(kohm) (ahs) (vah-ree-ahs) (noh-tahs) (moh-eh-dahs)*
now *with* *various*

no Brasil

dois reais *(heh-eyes)*

cinco reais *(heh-eyes)*

dez reais *(heh-eyes)*

cinqüenta reais *(seen-kwehn-tah)*

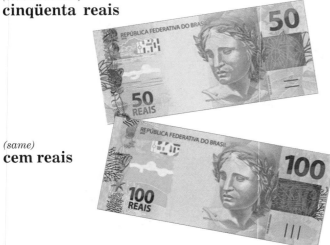

cem reais *(same)*

em Portugal

cinco euros *(seen-koo) (eh-oo-roosh)*

dez euros *(dehsh)*

vinte euros *(veen-chee)*

cinqüenta euros

Many English words that start with **sp** or **st** have an **e** in front of them in **português**.

- ❑ **a economia** *(eh-koh-noh-mee-ah)* . . . . economy
- ❑ **o espaço** *(es-pah-soo)* . . . . space
- ❑ **esplêndido** *(es-plehn-jee-doo)* . . . . splendid
- ❑ **o esporte** *(es-por-chee)* . . . . sport

e _____

_____

_____

_____

Review **os números dez** _(dehsh)_ through **mil** again. **Agora, como** _(koh-moo)_ do you say "twenty-two" **ou** _(oh)_ "fifty-three" **em português?** _(por-too-gaysh)_ Put the numbers together in a logical sequence just as you do in English. See if you can say **e** _(eh)_ write out **os números** on this **página.** _(pah-zhee-nah)_ page The answers **estão** _(es-town)_ are at the bottom of the **página.** _(pah-zhee-nah)_

1. _VINTE E CINCO_
(25 = 20 and 5)

2. _OITENTA E TRES_
(83 = 80 and 3)

3. _QUARENTA E ~~SETE~~ SETE_
(47 = 40 and 7)

4. _noventa e seis_
(96 = 90 and 6)

Now, **como** would you say the following **em português?** _(por-too-gaysh)_

5. _EU TENHO OITENTA EUReS_
(I have 80 reais.)

6. _Nos TEMos SESENTA E DOIS EUReS_
(We have 72 reais.)

To ask how much something costs **em português,** _(por-too-gaysh)_ one asks — **Quanto custa isso?** _(kwahn-too) (koos-tah) (ees-soo)_

Now you try it. _QUANTO CUSTA ISSo?_
(How much does that cost?)

Answer the following questions based on the numbers in parentheses.

7. **Quanto custa isso?** _(kwahn-too) (koos-tah) (ees-soo)_ costs that (it) costs **Custa** _DEZ_ (10) **reais.** _(heh-eyes)_

8. **Quanto custa isso?** _(ees-soo) (koos-tah)_ **Custa** _VINTE_ (20) **reais.** _(heh-eyes)_

9. **Quanto custa o livro?** _(lee-vroo)_ book **O livro custa** _DEZ E SETE_ (17) **reais.**

10. **Quanto custa o cartão postal?** _(kar-town) (pohs-tahl)_ postcard **O cartão postal custa** _DoIS_ (2) **reais.** _(kar-town) (pohs-tahl)_

(oh-zhee) *(ah-mahn-yahn)* *(ohn-tame)*
Hoje, Amanhã e Ontem
today   tomorrow   and   yesterday

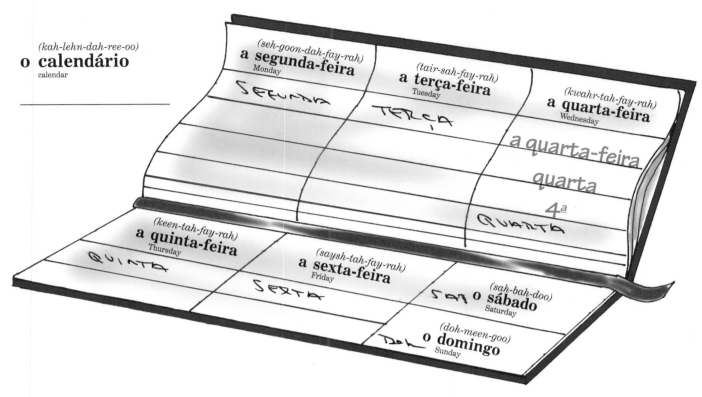

(kah-lehn-dah-ree-oo)
o calendário
calendar

(seh-goon-dah-fay-rah)
a segunda-feira
Monday

(tair-sah-fay-rah)
a terça-feira
Tuesday

(kwahr-tah-fay-rah)
a quarta-feira
Wednesday

(keen-tah-fay-rah)
a quinta-feira
Thursday

(saysh-tah-fay-rah)
a sexta-feira
Friday

(sah-bah-doo)
o sábado
Saturday

(doh-meen-goo)
o domingo
Sunday

(kah-lehn-dah-ree-oo) *(eh)*
Learn the days of the week by writing them in **o calendário** above **e** then move on to the

(kwah-troo) *(jee-ah)* *(fay-rah)*
quatro parts to each **dia.** Often **"feira"** is dropped when referring to the days of the week. You
four   day

(ohs) *(jee-ahs)*
will also see **os dias** abbreviated simply as <u>**dom.**</u>, <u>**2ª**</u>, <u>**3ª**</u>, <u>**4ª**</u>, <u>**5ª**</u>, <u>**6ª**</u> and <u>**sab.**</u>
days

(mahn-yahn)
a manhã
morning

(tar-jee)
a tarde
afternoon

(noy-chee)
a noite
evening

(noy-chee)
a noite
night

❑ **a estabilidade** *(es-tah-bee-lee-dah-jee)* .... stability		_____
❑ **a estação** *(es-tah-sown)* .... station		_____
❑ **o estado** *(es-tah-doo)* .... state	**e**	_____
❑ **a estátua** *(es-tah-too-ah)* .... statue		_____
❑ **o/a estudante** *(es-too-dahn-chee)* .... student		_____

It is **muito importante** *(mwee-too) (eem-por-tahn-chee)* to know the days of the week **e** *(eh)* the various parts of the day as well as these **três palavras** *(traysh) (pah-lah-vrahs)*.

very important

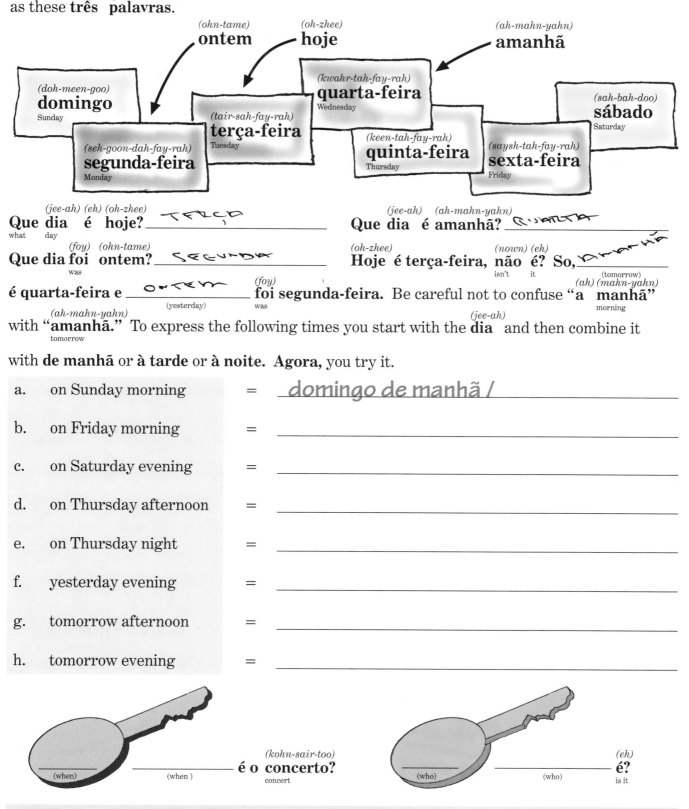

(ohn-tame) **ontem**

(oh-zhee) **hoje**

(ah-mahn-yahn) **amanhã**

domingo *(doh-meen-goo)*
Sunday

segunda-feira *(seh-goon-dah-fay-rah)*
Monday

terça-feira *(tair-sah-fay-rah)*
Tuesday

quarta-feira *(kwahr-tah-fay-rah)*
Wednesday

quinta-feira *(keen-tah-fay-rah)*
Thursday

sexta-feira *(saysh-tah-fay-rah)*
Friday

sábado *(sah-bah-doo)*
Saturday

Que dia é hoje? *(jee-ah) (eh) (oh-zhee)* ___TERÇA___
what day

Que dia é amanhã? *(jee-ah) (ah-mahn-yahn)* ___QUARTA___

Que dia foi ontem? *(foy) (ohn-tame)* ___SEGUNDA___
was

Hoje é terça-feira, não é? *(oh-zhee) (nown) (eh)* So,___Amanhã___
isn't it

é quarta-feira e ___ONTEM___ *(yesterday)* **foi segunda-feira.** *(foy)* Be careful not to confuse "**a manhã**" *(ah) (mahn-yahn)*
was morning (tomorrow)

with "**amanhã**." *(ah-mahn-yahn)* To express the following times you start with the **dia** *(jee-ah)* and then combine it
tomorrow

with **de manhã** or **à tarde** or **à noite**. **Agora,** you try it.

a.	on Sunday morning	=	*domingo de manhã /*
b.	on Friday morning	=	
c.	on Saturday evening	=	
d.	on Thursday afternoon	=	
e.	on Thursday night	=	
f.	yesterday evening	=	
g.	tomorrow afternoon	=	
h.	tomorrow evening	=	

___(when)___ ___(when)___ **é o concerto?** *(kohn-sair-too)*
concert

___(who)___ ___(who)___ **é?** *(eh)*
is it

ANSWERS

a. **domingo de manhã**
b. **sexta-feira de manhã**
c. **sábado à noite**
d. **quinta-feira à tarde**
e. **quinta-feira à noite**
f. **ontem à noite**
g. **amanhã à tarde**
h. **amanhã à noite**

Knowing the parts of **o dia** *(jee-ah)* / day will help you to learn the various **portugueses** *(por-too-gay-zeesh)* greetings below.

Practice these every day until your trip.

(bohm) (jee-ah)
bom dia _____
good morning / good day

(boh-ah)(tar-jee)
boa tarde _____
good   afternoon

(boh-ah)(noy-chee)
boa noite _____
good evening / good night

Take the next **três** *(traysh)* labels **e** stick them on the appropriate things in your **casa.** *(kah-zah)* / house Make sure you

attach them to the correct items, as they are only **em português.** *(por-too-gaysh)* How about the bathroom

mirror for "**bom dia**" *(bohm)*? **ou** *(oh)* / or your alarm clock for "**boa noite**" *(noy-chee)*? Let's not forget,

(oi) (oh-lah)
oi / olá _____
hello / hi

(chow) (ah-deh-oos)
tchau / adeus _____
good-bye

Como vai *(vy)*? _____
how are you

Tudo bem *(too-doo) (bame)*? _____
how's it going

Now for some "**sim** *(seem)* / yes" or "**não** *(nown)* / no" questions –

Is the sky **azul** *(ah-zool)*? _____   Is your car **marrom** *(mar-hohm)*? _____

Is your favorite color **vermelho** *(vair-mel-yoo)*? _____   Is today **sábado** *(sah-bah-doo)*? _____

Do you own a **cachorro** *(kah-shor-hoo)*? _____   Do you own a **gato** *(gah-too)*? _____

You are about one-fourth of your way through this **livro e** *(book)* it is a good time to quickly review **as**

palavras you have learned before doing the crossword puzzle on the next **página.** *(pah-zhee-nah)* Have fun **e**

(boh-ah) (sor-chee)
boa sorte!
good   luck

ANSWERS TO THE CROSSWORD PUZZLE

ACROSS		DOWN			
1. custa	18. dez	37. janela	1. calma	11. nós	24. sala	39. seis
3. bicicleta	21. estado	38. um	2. tapete	13. selos	26. eu	40. casa
6. mesa	23. hoje	40. chocolate	3. banco	14. ingresso	27. por que	41. como
7. sim	25. correspondência	42. noite	4. cheque	16. doutor	29. rosa	43. de
8. quem	28. abril	43. dia	5. cadeira	17. trem	30. marrom
10. tenho	32. real	44. ontem	7. segunda-	19. zero	31. cachorro
12. inglês	33. amanhã	45. três	feira	20. cozinha	34. menina
15. telefone	35. salada	46. ativo	9. treze	22. trinta	36. sábado

24

PALAVRAS CRUZADAS
(kroo-zah-dahs)
crossword puzzle

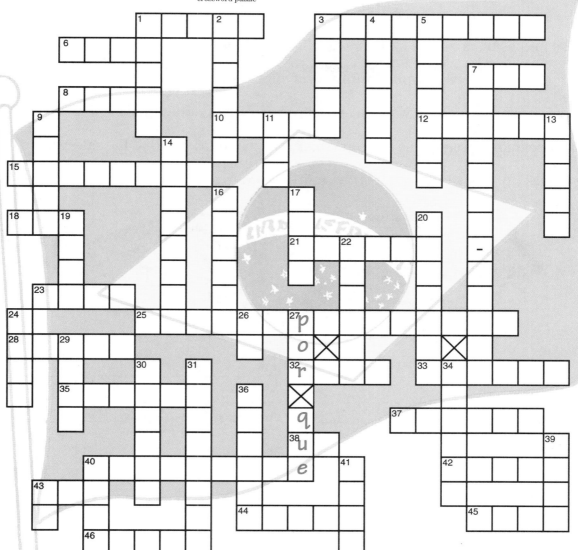

ACROSS

1. (it) costs
3. bicycle
6. table
7. yes
8. who
10. (I) have
12. English
15. telephone
18. ten
21. state
23. today
25. mail
28. April
32. Brazilian currency
33. tomorrow
35. salad
37. window
38. one
40. chocolate
42. night
43. day
44. yesterday
45. three
46. active

DOWN

1. calm
2. rug
3. bank
4. check
5. chair
7. Monday
9. thirteen
11. we
13. stamps
14. ticket
16. doctor (title)
17. train
19. zero
20. kitchen
22. thirty
24. living room
26. I
27. why
29. pink
30. brown
31. dog
34. girl
36. Saturday
39. six
40. house
41. how
43. of, from

❏ **elétrico** *(eh-leh-tree-koo)* .... electric _____
❏ **enorme** *(eh-nor-mee)* .... enormous _____
❏ **entrar** *(ehn-trar)* .... to enter **e** _____
❏ **o erro** *(air-hoo)* .... error _____
❏ **o e-mail** *(ee-may-oo)* .... email _____

Portuguese prepositions (words like "in," "on," "through" and "next to") **são** *(sown)* / are easy to learn, **e**

they allow you to be **preciso** *(preh-see-zoo)* / precise **com** a **mínimo** *(mee-nee-moo)* / minimum of effort. Instead of having to point **quatro** *(kwah-troo)* times

at a piece of yummy pastry you would like, you can explain precisely which one you want by

saying **está** *(it) is* behind, in front of, next to **ou** *(oh)* under the piece of pastry that the salesperson is

starting to pick up. Let's learn some of these little **palavras**

(ehm)
em _____
into / in

(dee)
de* _____
of / from

(soh-bree)
sobre _____
over / on / on top of

(ehm-by-shoo) (dee)   *(ah-by-shoo)*
embaixo de* / **abaixo** _____
under   below

(ehn-tree)
entre _____ *entre, entre, entre* _____
between

(ehm) (frehn-chee) (dee)
em frente de* _____
in   front   of

(ah-trahs)
atrás _____
behind

(doo) (lah-doo) (dee)
do lado de* _____
next to

(pah-rah)
para _____
to

    (boh-loo)   (tor-tah)   (doh-see)
o bolo, a torta, o doce _____
cake,   pie,   pastry!

* The pronunciation for **"de"** varies. You'll hear *(dee)*, *(jee)*, *(deh)* and *(jeh)*. The differences are

very subtle. Note that **"de"** can combine with **"a"** or **"o"** to form **"da"** *(de+a)* / the and **"do. "** *(de+o)* / the Also, **"em"** from the   *(ehm)* from the

combines with **"a"** or **"o"** to become **"na"** *(em+a)* / in the or **"no."** *(em+o)* / in the

_____ _____ **vai?** *(vy)*
(how)   (how)   are you

_____ _____ **o táxi é amarelo?** *(tahk-see) (ah-mah-reh-loo)*
(why)   (why)   yellow

❑ **exato** *(eh-zah-too)*	exact	_____
❑ **excelente** *(eh-seh-lehn-chee)*	excellent	_____
❑ **a experiência** *(es-peh-ree-ayn-see-ah)*	experience **e**	_____
❑ **o extremo** *(es-treh-moo)*	extreme	_____
❑ **a expressão** *(es-prehs-sown)*	expression	_____

(doh-see)
O doce está _____ **a mesa.**
pastry — (on) — table

(kah-shor-hoo) (preh-too)
O cachorro preto está _____ **mesa.**
dog — (under the)

(meh-jee-koo)
O médico está _____ *(oh-tel)* **hotel** *(noh-voo)* **novo.**
doctor — (in the) — new

(ohn-jee)
Onde está o médico? _____

(oh-mehn)
O homem está _____ **casa.**
man — (in front of the)

(oh-mehn)
Onde está o homem? _____

(teh-leh-foh-nee)
O telefone está _____ *(por-tah)* **porta.**
telephone — (next to the) — door

Onde está o telefone? _____

Agora fill in each blank on the picture below with the best possible one of these *(peh-kay-nahs)* **pequenas**
now — little

palavras. Will you be attending **um jogo** *(zhoh-goo) (deh)* **de** *(foo-cheh-bohl)* **futebol** while abroad? **Maracanã** *(mah-rah-kah-nahn)* **no Rio** is
soccer game

the largest stadium in South America **e** was built for the 1950 World Cup Championship.

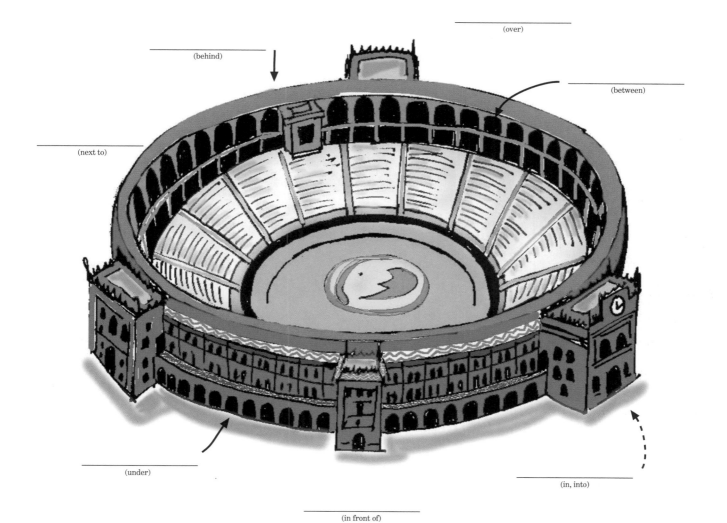

(over)

(behind)

(between)

(next to)

(under)

(in, into)

(in front of)

❑ **a fama** *(fah-mah)* .... fame		_____
❑ **a família** *(fah-mee-lee-ah)* .... family	**f**	_____
❑ **famoso** *(fah-moh-zoo)* .... famous		_____
❑ **o favor** *(fah-vor)* .... favor		_____
– **(por favor)** = for a favor .... please		_____

You have learned **os dias** *(jee-ahs)* **da semana,** *(seh-mah-nah)* so now **é hora** *(oh-rah)* to learn os **mêses** *(may-zeesh)* **do ano** *(doo)(ah-noo)* **e** all the days   of the week   it is time   months   of the year

different kinds of **tempo.** *(tame-poo)*
weather

(zhah-nay-roo)
janeiro

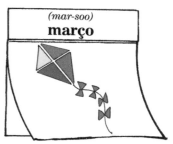

(feh-veh-ray-roo)
fevereiro

(mar-soo)
março

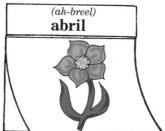

(ah-breel)
abril

(my-oo)
maio

(zhoon-yoo)
junho

(zhool-yoo)
julho

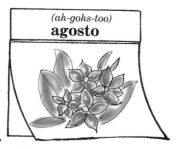

(ah-gohs-too)
agosto

(seh-tem-broo)
setembro

(oh-too-broo)
outubro

(noh-vem-broo)
novembro

(deh-zem-broo)
dezembro

When someone asks, "**Como está o tempo hoje?**" *(koh-moo) (es-tah) (tame-poo) (oh-zhee)* you have a variety of answers. Let's learn
how   is   the weather   today

them but first, does this sound familiar?

Trinta *(treen-tah)* **dias** *(jee-ahs)* **tem** *(tame)* **setembro,** *(seh-tem-broo)* **abril,** *(ah-breel)* **junho** *(zhoon-yoo)* **e** *(eh)* **novembro**...
has

☐ **o festival** *(fehs-chee-vahl)* .... festival		_____
☐ **a figura** *(fee-goo-rah)* .... figure		_____
☐ **o final** *(fee-nahl)* .... final	**f**	_____
☐ **o folclore** *(fohl-kloh-ree)* .... folklore		_____
☐ **a forma** *(for-mah)* .... form		_____

(tame-poo) *(oh-zhee)*
Como está o tempo hoje? _____
how   is   today

(neh-vah)(ehm) (zhah-nay-roo)
Neva em janeiro. _____
it snows   in

(tahm-bame)   (feh-veh-ray-roo)
Neva também em fevereiro. _____
         also

(shoh-vee)   (mar-soo)
Chove em março. _____
it rains

(tahm-bame)
Chove também em abril. _____

(vehn-tah)   (my-oo)
Venta em maio. _____
it is windy

(tahm-bame)   (zhoon-yoo)
Venta também em junho. _____

(fahs) (kah-lor)   (zhool-yoo)
Faz calor em julho. _____
it makes heat (= it is hot)

(fahs)   (ah-gohs-too)
Faz calor também em agosto. _____

(bohm) (tame-poo)   (seh-tem-broo)
Faz bom tempo em setembro. _____
      good

(ah) (neh-voh-ah)   (oh-too-broo)
Há névoa em outubro. _____
there is fog

(fahs) (free-oh)
Faz frio em novembro. _____
      cold

(mow) (tame-poo)
Faz mau tempo em dezembro. _____
      bad

(oh-zhee)
Como está o tempo hoje? _____ *Chove hoje. Chove hoje. Chove hoje.*

(hee-oo)
Como está o tempo no Rio? _____

Como está o tempo no Brasil? _____

Como está o tempo em Portugal? _____

❏ **a fortuna** *(for-too-nah)*	fortune		_____
❏ **a fotografia** *(foh-toh-grah-fee-ah)*	photograph		_____
❏ **freqüente** *(freh-kwehn-chee)*	frequent	**f**	_____
❏ **a fruta** *(froo-tah)*	fruit		_____
❏ **o futuro** *(foo-too-roo)*	future		_____

Agora for the seasons *(doo)* **do** *(ah-noo)* **ano** . . .
of the year

(een-vair-noo)
o inverno
winter

(veh-rown)
o verão
summer

(oh-toh-noo)
o outono
autumn

(pree-mah-veh-rah)
a primavera
spring

(sehn-chee-grah-doo)
Centígrado
Centigrade

(fah-rehn-heit)
Fahrenheit
Fahrenheit

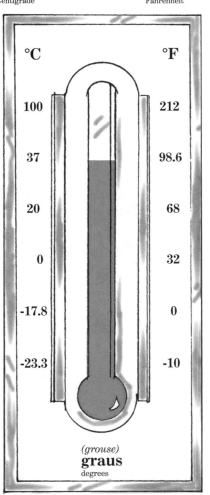

°C   °F

100   212

37   98.6

20   68

0   32

-17.8   0

-23.3   -10

(grouse)
graus
degrees

Remember that the seasons **no Brasil** are opposite those in North America as **Brasil** is in the southern hemisphere.

At this point, **é uma** *(oo-mah)* **boa idéia** *(ee-day-ah)* to familiarize
good idea
yourself **com as temperaturas.** *(tame-peh-rah-too-rahs)* Carefully study
temperatures
o termômetro *(tair-moh-meh-troo)* because **as temperaturas** *(tame-peh-rah-too-rahs)* **no**
Brasil e em Portugal *(brah-zeel)* *(por-too-gahl)* are calculated on the basis of Centigrade (not Fahrenheit).

To convert °F to °C, subtract 32 and multiply by 0.55.

98.6 °F - 32 = 66.6 x 0.55 = 37 °C

To convert °C to °F, multiply by 1.8 and add 32.

37 °C x 1.8 = 66.6 + 32 = 98.6 °F

What is normal body temperature in **Centígrado?** *(sehn-chee-grah-doo)*

What is the freezing point in **Centígrado?**

(kah-zah) *(fah-mee-lee-ah)* *(heh-lee-zhee-own)*
Casa, Família e Religião
home   family   religion

(noh) *(brah-zeel)*
No Brasil, not just the parents, but also the grandparents, aunts, uncles and cousins are all

(fah-mee-lee-ah) *(doh-nah)*
considered as close **família.**   Study the family tree below. Brazilians use **"dona"** when
family

(oh)
addressing a woman as Miss, Mrs. **ou** as a general reflection of respect (**Dona Lucia Faria** or

(sehn-yoh-rah) *(sehn-yor)*
Senhora Faria). For men, you would use **"senhor"** (**Senhor Faria**).
Mrs.   Mr.

Maria Berti Faria
a avó
grandmother

Augusto Rio Faria
o avô
grandfather

Orlando Berti Faria
o pai
father

Alice Faria Pires
a tia
aunt

Lucia da Costa Faria
a mãe
mother

Hugo Rebello Pires
o tio
uncle

Mickael da Costa Faria
o filho
son

Marcela da Costa Faria
a filha
daughter

❏ **habitual** *(ah-bee-too-ahl)*	habitual	
❏ **a história** *(ees-toh-ree-ah)*	history	
❏ **honesto** *(oh-nehs-too)*	honest, decent	**h**
❏ **a honra** *(ohn-hah)*	honor	
❏ **o humor** *(oo-mor)*	humor	

Let's learn how to identify **a família** *(fah-mee-lee-ah)* by **nome** *(noh-mee)*. Study the following **exemplos** *(eh-zame-ploosh)* carefully.

family   name   examples

(kwahl) (eh) (seh-oo) (noh-mee)
Qual é o seu nome? _____
what is your name

(meh-oo) (noh-mee) (eh)
Meu nome é _____.
my name is   (your name)

(piesh)
os pais
parents

(pie)
o pai _____
father

(kwahl) (noh-mee) (doo) (pie)
Qual é o nome do pai? _____
what name of the father

(mah-een)
a mãe _____
mother

(dah) (mah-een)
Qual é o nome da mãe? _____
what of the mother

(feel-yoosh)
os filhos
children

(feel-yoo) *(feel-yah)* *(eer-mown)* *(eer-mahn)*
o filho e a filha = irmão e irmã
brother sister

(feel-yoo)
o filho _____
son

(kwahl) (noh-mee) (doo)
Qual é o nome do filho? _____
what name son

(feel-yah)
a filha _____
daughter

Qual é o nome da filha? _____
daughter

(pah-rehn-cheesh)
os parentes
relatives

(ah-voh)
o avô _____
grandfather

(doo) (ah-voh)
Qual é o nome do avô? _____
grandfather

(ah-voh)
a avó _____
grandmother

Qual é o nome da avó? _____
grandmother

Now you ask —

_____
(What is your name?)

And answer —

_____
(My name is . . .)

(koh-zeen-yah)
A Cozinha
kitchen

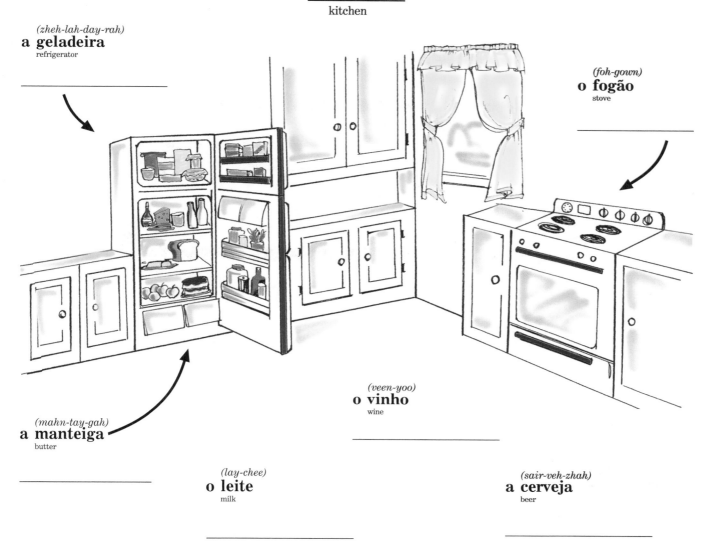

(zheh-lah-day-rah)
a geladeira
refrigerator

(foh-gown)
o fogão
stove

(veen-yoo)
o vinho
wine

(mahn-tay-gah)
a manteiga
butter

(lay-chee)
o leite
milk

(sair-veh-zhah)
a cerveja
beer

Answer these questions aloud.

(ohn-jee) *(sair-veh-zhah)*
Onde está a cerveja? . . . . **A cerveja está na geladeira.**
beer *(ah)* *(zheh-lah-day-rah)*

(lay-chee)
Onde está o leite?
milk

(veen-yoo)
Onde está o vinho?
wine

(mahn-tay-gah)
Onde está a manteiga?
butter

(ah-brah) *(lee-vroo)* *(pah-zhee-nahs)*
Agora abra your **livro** to the **páginas** **com** the labels **e** remove the next group of labels **e**
open book

(koy-zahs) *(koh-zeen-yah)*
proceed to label all these **coisas** in your **cozinha.**
things kitchen

❏	**a influência** *(een-floo-ayn-see-ah)*	influence	
❏	**a informação** *(een-for-mah-sown)*	information	**i**
❏	**inglês** *(een-glaysh)*	English	
❏	**a instrução** *(een-stroo-sown)*	instruction	
❏	**o instrumento** *(een-stroo-mehn-too)*	instrument	

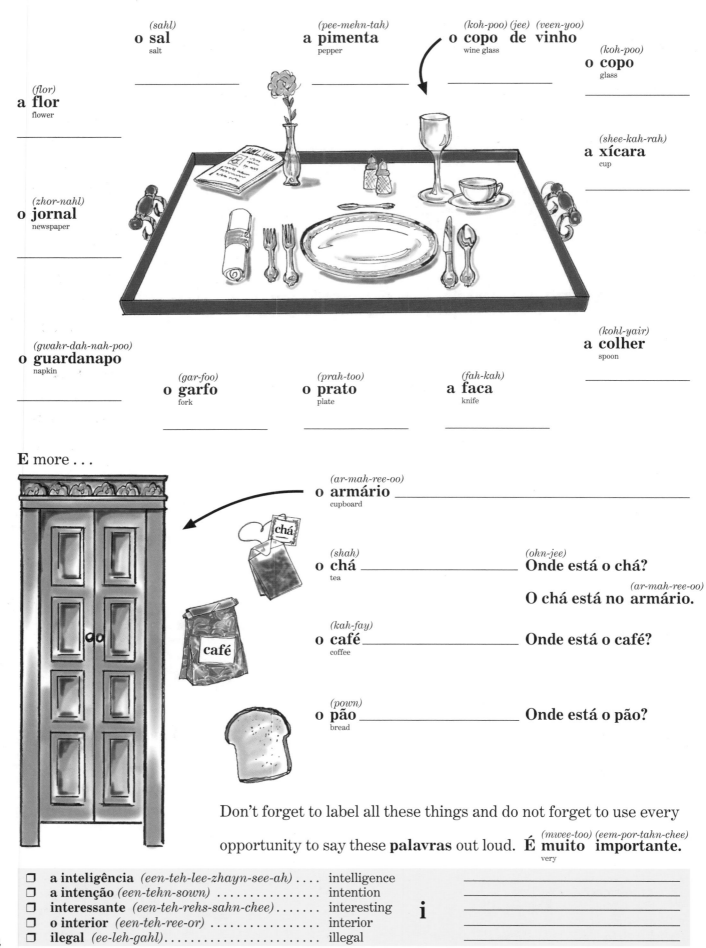

(sahl)
o sal
salt

(pee-mehn-tah)
a pimenta
pepper

(koh-poo) (jee) (veen-yoo)
o copo de vinho
wine glass

(koh-poo)
o copo
glass

(flor)
a flor
flower

(shee-kah-rah)
a xícara
cup

(zhor-nahl)
o jornal
newspaper

(kohl-yair)
a colher
spoon

(gwahr-dah-nah-poo)
o guardanapo
napkin

(gar-foo)
o garfo
fork

(prah-too)
o prato
plate

(fah-kah)
a faca
knife

E more . . .

(ar-mah-ree-oo)
o armário _____
cupboard

(shah)
o chá _____
tea

(ohn-jee)
Onde está o chá?

(ar-mah-ree-oo)
O chá está no armário.

(kah-fay)
o café _____
coffee

Onde está o café?

(pown)
o pão _____
bread

Onde está o pão?

Don't forget to label all these things and do not forget to use every

opportunity to say these **palavras** out loud. **É muito importante.**
(mwee-too) (eem-por-tahn-chee)
very

❏	**a inteligência** *(een-teh-lee-zhayn-see-ah)*	intelligence	_____
❏	**a intenção** *(een-tehn-sown)*	intention	_____
❏	**interessante** *(een-teh-rehs-sahn-chee)*	interesting **i**	_____
❏	**o interior** *(een-teh-ree-or)*	interior	_____
❏	**ilegal** *(ee-leh-gahl)*	illegal	_____

(dehs-kool-pee)
desculpe

(seh-loo)
o selo

(kar-town) *(pohs-tahl)*
o cartão postal

(pahs-sah-por-chee)
o passaporte

(kah-zah-koo)
o casaco

(kah-mee-zeh-tah)
a camiseta

(mah-lah)
a mala

(gwahr-dah-shoo-vah)
o guarda-chuva

(koo-eh-kah)
a cueca

(dehs-pair-tah-dor)
o despertador

(pahs-sah-zhame)
a passagem

(kah-pah) *(shoo-vah)*
a capa de chuva

(vehs-chee-doo)
o vestido

(bohl-sah)
a bolsa

(loo-vahs)
as luvas

(bloo-zah)
a blusa

(kar-tay-rah)
a carteira

(sy-ah)
a saia

(jeen-yay-roo)
o dinheiro

(soo-eh-tair)
o suéter

(kar-toynsh) *(kreh-jee-too)*
os cartões de crédito

(kohm-bee-nah-sown)
a combinação

(sheck-esh) *(vee-ah-zhame)*
os cheques de viagem

(soo-chee-own)
o sutiã

(lah-peesh)
o lápis

(mah-key-nah) *(foh-toh-grah-fee-kah)*
a maquina fotografica

(kahl-seen-yah)
a calcinha

(teh-leh-vee-zown)
a televisão

(feel-mee)
o filme

(may-ahs)
as meias

(kah-neh-tah)
a caneta

(may-ah-kahl-sah)
a meia-calça

(heh-vees-tah)
a revista

(pee-zhah-mah)
o pijama

(lee-vroo)
o livro

(kah-mee-zoh-lah)
a camisola

(kohm-poo-tah-dor)
o computador

(oh-koo-loosh) *(sohl)*
os óculos de sol

(oh-koo-loosh)
os óculos

(pah-pel)
o papel

(eh-oo) *(soh)*
Eu sou de _____.

(kair-oo) *(ah-prehn-dair)* *(por-too-gaysh)*
Quero aprender português.

(meh-oo) *(noh-mee)* *(eh)*
Meu nome é _____.

(kar-tah)
a carta

PLUS . . .

This book includes a number of other innovative features unique to the *"10 minutes a day*®*"* Series. At the back of this book, you will find twelve pages of flash cards. Cut them out and flip through them at least once a day.

On pages 116, 117 and 118 you will find a beverage guide and a menu guide. Don't wait until your trip to use them. Clip out the menu guide and use it tonight at the dinner table. Take them both with you the next time you dine at your favorite Portuguese restaurant.

By using the special features in this book, you will be speaking Portuguese before you know it.

(boh-ah) *(sor-chee)*
Boa sorte!
good luck

(heh-lee-zhee-own)
A Religião
religion

(brah-zeel)   *(vah-ree-eh-dah-jee)*   *(heh-lee-zhee-oynsh)*

No Brasil there is a wide **variedade** of accepted **religiões.** However, a person is usually
                          variety   religions

one of the following.

(kah-toh-lee-koo) (kah-toh-lee-kah)

1. **católico / católica** _____
   Catholic (♂)   Catholic (♀)

(proh-tehs-tahn-chee)

2. **protestante** _____
   Protestant (♂)/(♀)

(zhoo-deh-oo) (zhoo-jee-ah)

3. **judeu / judia** _____
   Jewish (♂)   Jewish (♀)

(oo-mah) (ee-greh-zhah) (brah-zee-lay-rah)

É uma igreja brasileira? Sim!
is it   church
          (ee-greh-zhah)

É uma igreja católica?
          (ee-greh-zhah)

É uma igreja protestante?
          (ee-greh-zhah) (noh-vah)

É uma igreja nova?
                new
          (vel-yah)

É uma igreja velha?
              old

(por-too-gaysh)

There are different ways to say "I am" **em português:**

(eh-oo) (soh)   *(es-toh)*

eu sou _____   **eu estou** _____
I   am   I   am

(eh-oo) (soh)

Use "**eu sou**" when you are telling your profession, religion, gender or a more permanent fact

(eh-oo) (es-toh)

about yourself such as your nationality. Use "**eu estou**" when you are telling something

(eh-oo) (es-toh) (bame)

temporary such as your location or how you feel, for example, "**Eu estou bem,**" or simply,
                                                    I   am   well

(bame)

"**Estou bem.**" Test yourself – write each sentence on the next page for more practice. Add your
(I) am   well

own personal variations as well.

(ees-soo)

_____ _____ **custa isso?**
(how much)   (how much)   this

❑ **a jaqueta** *(zhah-kay-tah)* . . . . jacket		_____
❑ **o/a jornalista** *(zhor-nah-lees-tah)*. . . . . journalist		_____
❑ **julho** *(zhool-yoo)* . . . . July	**j**	_____
❑ **junho** *(zhoon-yoo)* . . . . June		_____
❑ **juvenil** *(zhoo-veh-neel)* . . . . juvenile		_____

(soh) (kah-toh-lee-koo)
Eu sou católico. ____________________
I am Catholic (♂)

(kah-toh-lee-kah)
Sou católica. ____________________
(I) am Catholic (♀)

(soh) (zhoo-deh-oo)
Sou judeu. ____________________
Jewish (♂)

(zhoo-jee-ah)
Sou judia. ____________________
Jewish (♀)

(es-toh) (eh-oo-roh-pah)
Eu estou na Europa. ____________________
Europe

(ee-greh-zhah)
Estou na igreja. ____________________
church

(es-toh) (oh-tel)
Estou no hotel. ____________________
in the

(foh-mee)
Estou com fome. ____________________
with hunger (= I am hungry)

(soh) (proh-tehs-tahn-chee)
Sou protestante. ____________________
(I) am Protestant (♂) and (♀)

(ah-meh-ree-kah-noo)
Sou americano. ____________________
American (♂)

(kah-nah-dehn-see)
Sou canadense. ____________________
Canadian (♂) and (♀)

(es-toh) (hee-oo)
Estou no Rio. ____________________
(I) am in

(sown) (pow-loo)
Estou em São Paulo. ____________________
in

(por-too-gahl)
Estou em Portugal. ____________________

(hehs-tow-rahn-chee)
Estou no restaurante. ____________________

(seh-jee)
Estou com sede. ____________________
with thirst (= I am thirsty)

To negate any statement, simply add "**<u>não</u>**" *(nown)* (not / no) before the verb.

(nown) (proh-tehs-tahn-chee)
<u>Não</u> sou protestante. ____________________
(I) am not

(nown) (es-toh) (seh-jee)
<u>Não</u> estou com sede. ____________________
(I) am not

Go through and drill these sentences again but using "**não**" *(nown)*. **Agora**, take a piece of paper. Our **família** *(fah-mee-lee-ah)* from earlier had a reunion. Identify everyone below by writing **a palavra portuguesa** *(por-too-gay-zah)* **correta** *(kor-heh-tah)* (correct) for each person — **a mãe** *(mah-een)*, **o tio** and so on. Don't forget **o cachorro** *(kah-shor-hoo)*!

❒ **legal** *(leh-gahl)*	legal		____________
– **legal** = used as slang	cool		____________
❒ **a lição** *(lee-sown)*	lesson	**l**	____________
❒ **o licor** *(lee-kor)*	liquor		____________
❒ **o limão** *(lee-mown)*	lime		____________

(ah-prehn-dair)
Aprender!
to learn

(doysh)
You have already used **dois** very important verbs: **eu** *(kair-oo)* **quero** and **eu** *(tehn-yoo)* **tenho**. Although you might
   I   want   I   have

be able to get by with only these verbs, let's assume you want to do better. First a quick review.

How do you say ▢ **"I"** em *(por-too-gaysh)* **português?** _____

How do you say ▢ **"we"** em **português?** _____

(doysh) *(mwee-too)*
Compare these **dois** charts **muito** carefully **e** learn these **palavras** now.
              two   very

I = **eu** *(eh-oo)* _____	we = **nós** *(noys)* _____
you = **você** *(voh-say)* _____	you (plural) = **vocês** *(voh-saysh)* _____
he = **ele** *(eh-lee)* _____	they = **eles** *(eh-leesh)* (🧍 or mixed) _____
she = **ela** *(eh-lah)* _____	they = **elas** *(eh-lahs)* (🧍) _____

(een-glay-zahs) *(por-too-gay-zahs)*
Not too hard, is it? Draw lines between the matching **palavras inglesas e portuguesas** below

to see if you can keep these **palavras** straight in your mind.

(noys)
nós   I

(eh-leesh)
eles   they (🧍)

(eh-lee)
ele   we

eu   he

(voh-say)
você   you

ela   she

(eh-lahs)
elas   they (🧍)

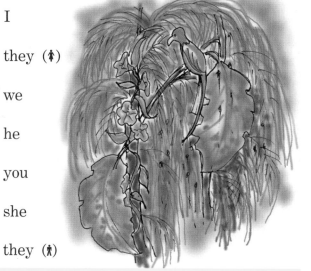

❏ **a limonada** *(lee-moh-nah-dah)*	lemonade	_____
❏ **a lista** *(lees-tah)*	list	_____
❏ **o litro** *(lee-troo)*	liter	**l** _____
❏ **local** *(loh-kahl)*	local	_____
❏ **longo** *(lohn-goo)*	long	_____

Agora close **o livro** *(lee-vroo)* **e** write out both columns of this practice on a piece of **papel**. *(pah-pel)* How did **você** *(voh-say)*
do? **Bem ou mal?** *(bame)* *(mahl)* **Agora** that **você** *(voh-say)* know these **palavras, você** can say almost anything **em**
português *(por-too-gaysh)* with one basic formula: the "plug-in" formula.

To demonstrate, let's take **seis** *(saysh)* basic **e** practical verbs **e** see how the "plug-in" formula works.

Write the verbs in the blanks after **você** *(voh-say)* have practiced saying them out loud many times.

(fah-lar) **falar** to speak	_____	*(kair-air)* **querer** to want	_____
(kohm-prar) **comprar** to buy	*comprar, comprar*	*(tair)* **ter** to have	_____
(ahn-dar) **andar** to walk	_____	*(veer)* **vir** to come	_____

Besides the familiar words already circled, can **você** find the above verbs in the puzzle below?

When **você** find them, write them in the blanks to the right.

A	R	O	H	A	F	I	J	X	T	N
F	A	L	A	R	I	T	A	R	E	O
D	N	D	U	O	Q	U	E	M	T	C
A	D	C	O	M	P	R	A	R	E	E
R	A	M	E	Q	U	E	R	E	R	U
O	R	D	V	X	U	T	S	E	I	S
V	E	N	I	R	L	E	B	I	E	L
X	O	A	R	S	E	D	O	N	D	E

1. _____

2. _____

3. _____

4. _____

5. _____

6. _____

❏ **mágico** *(mah-zhee-koo)*	magic	
❏ **maio** *(my-oo)*	May	
❏ **o mapa** *(mah-pah)*	map	**m**
❏ **a máquina** *(mah-kee-nah)*	machine	
❏ **a marca** *(mar-kah)*	mark	

Study the following patterns carefully.

(eh-oo) **eu**			
	fal<u>o</u>	=	I *speak*
	compr<u>o</u>	=	I *buy*
	and<u>o</u>	=	I *walk*
	quer<u>o</u>	=	I *want*
	tenh<u>o</u>*	=	I *have*
	venh<u>o</u>*	=	I *come*

(noys) **nós**			
	fal<u>amos</u>	=	we *speak*
	compr<u>amos</u>	=	we *buy*
	and<u>amos</u>	=	we *walk*
	quer<u>emos</u>	=	we *want*
	t<u>emos</u>	=	we *have*
	v<u>imos</u>	=	we *come*

Note:
- With all these verbs, the first thing you do is drop the final "**ar**," "**er**," or "**ir**" from the basic verb form or stem.

- With "**eu**," add "**o**" to the basic verb form. ***** Some verbs are irregular. Think of "**o**" as the ending to go with "**eu**."

- With "**nós**," add the vowel of the original ending plus "**mos**" (a+mos, e+mos, i+mos).

* Some verbs just will not conform to the pattern! Do your best to learn them, but don't let them surprise you and don't worry. Speak slowly **e** clearly, **e** you will be perfectly understood whether you say "**eu veno**" or "**eu venho**." Portuguese speakers will be delighted that you have taken the time to learn their language.

Note:
- Portuguese has many different ways of saying "you" whereas in English we only use one word.

- *(voh-say)* "**Você**" will be used throughout this book and will be appropriate for most situations. "**Você**" refers to one person.
  you

- "**Vocês**" refers to more than one person both in a formal and informal sense, as we
  you (plural)
  might say, "you all."

- "**Tu**" is a familiar form of address used primarily in Portugal as well as in some parts
  you (singular)
  of Brasil and is generally reserved for family members and very close friends.

❏ **março** *(mar-soo)*	March	
❏ **masculino** *(mahs-koo-lee-noo)*	masculine	**m**
❏ **a matemática** *(mah-teh-mah-chee-kah)*	mathematics	
❏ **o matrimônio** *(mah-tree-moh-nee-oo)*	matrimony	
❏ **o mecânico** *(meh-kah-nee-koo)*	mechanic	

Here's your next group of patterns!

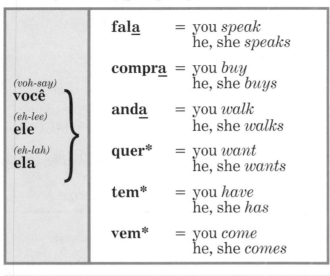

(voh-say) **você** *(eh-lee)* **ele** *(eh-lah)* **ela** }	**fal<u>a</u>**	=	you *speak* he, she *speaks*
	compr<u>a</u>	=	you *buy* he, she *buys*
	and<u>a</u>	=	you *walk* he, she *walks*
	quer*	=	you *want* he, she *wants*
	tem*	=	you *have* he, she *has*
	vem*	=	you *come* he, she *comes*

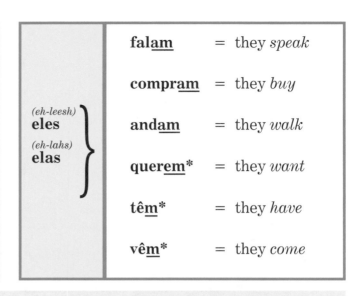

(eh-leesh) **eles** *(eh-lahs)* **elas** }	**fal<u>am</u>**	=	they *speak*
	compr<u>am</u>	=	they *buy*
	and<u>am</u>	=	they *walk*
	quer<u>em</u>*	=	they *want*
	tê<u>m</u>*	=	they *have*
	vê<u>m</u>*	=	they *come*

Note: • Again drop the final **"ar," "er,"** or **"ir"** from the basic verb form or stem.

• With **"você," "ele"** and **"ela,"** add **"a"** if the original ending was **"ar"** and **"e"** if the original ending was **"er"** or **"ir"** unless its one of those non-conformist verbs.

• With **"eles,"** and **"elas"** simply add **"m"** to the **"você," "ele"** and **"ela"** form.

* Remember some verbs don't follow the patterns. Focus on the similarities.

(ah-key) (es-town) (saysh)
Aqui estão seis more verbs.
here   are   six

(ehn-trar)
entrar _____
to enter

(preh-see-zar) (dee)
precisar de _____
to need, to have need of

(ah-prehn-dair)
aprender _____
to learn

(vee-vair)
viver _____
to live

(vehn-dair)
vender _____
to sell

(heh-peh-cheer)
repetir _____
to repeat

(es-chee)
At the back of **este livro**, **você** will find twelve
           this

páginas of flash cards to help you learn these
pages

palavras novas. Cut them out; carry them in
        new

your briefcase, purse, pocket **ou** knapsack; **e**
          or

review them whenever **você** have a free moment.

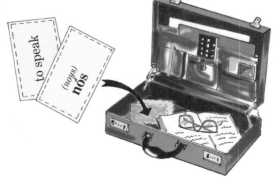

❑	**a medicina** *(meh-jee-see-nah)*	medicine	_____
❑	**o mediterrâneo** *(meh-jee-tair-hah-neh-oo)* . . .	Mediterranean	_____
❑	**a melodia** *(meh-loh-jee-ah)*	melody	**m** _____
❑	**o menu** *(meh-noo)*	menu	_____
❑	**o mercado** *(mair-kah-doo)*	market	_____

Agora, it is your turn to practice what **você** have learned. Fill in the following blanks with the correct form of the verb. Each time **você** write out the sentence, be sure to say it aloud.

(fah-lar)
falar
to speak

Bom dia!

Eu _____ *(por-too-gaysh)* **português.**

Você _____ *(een-glaysh)* **inglês.**

Ele _fala/_ _____ *(zhah-poh-naysh)* **japonês.**
Ela   Japanese

Nós _____ *(frahn-saysh)* **francês.**
                                                        French
                                                        (es-pahn-yohl)
Eles _____ **espanhol.**
Elas   Spanish

(kohm-prar)
comprar
to buy

Eu _____ **um livro.**
                                                        book
                                                        (heh-loh-zhee-oo)
Você _compra/_ _____ **um relógio.**
                                                        watch / clock

Ele _____ **uma salada.**
Ela

Nós _____ *(kar-hoo)* **um carro.**

(doysh) (een-grehs-soos)   *(teh-ah-troo)*
Eles _____ **dois ingressos de teatro.**
Elas   theater

(ahn-dar)
andar
to walk

Eu _ando/_ _____ *(pah-rah) (kah-zah)* **para a casa.**
                                                        to
Você _____ *(pry-ah)* **para a praia.**
                                                        beach

Ele _____ **para o hotel.**
Ela

Nós _____ **para o banco.**

Eles _____ *(bahn-yay-roosh)* **para os banheiros.**
Elas   restrooms

(kair-air)
querer
to want

Eu _____ *(koh-poo) (jee)* **um copo de vinho tinto.** *(cheen-too)*
                                                        red

Você _quer/_ _____ **um copo de vinho branco.**
                                                        white
                                                        (hoh-zay)
Ele _quer/_ _____ **um copo de vinho rosé.**
Ela   rosé

Nós _____ *(traysh)* **três copos de água.** *(ah-gwah)*
                                                        water
                                                        (soo-koo)
Eles _querem/_ _____ **cinco copos de suco.**
Elas   juice

(tair)
ter
to have

Eu _tenho/_ _____ *(keen-yehn-toosh) (heh-eyes)* **quinhentos reais.**

Você _tem/_ _____ *(doysh)* **dois mil reais.**

Ele _____ *(doh-lah-reesh)* **dez dólares   americanos.**
Ela

Nós _temos/_ _____ *(heh-eyes)* **reais.**

Eles _têm/_ _____ *(doh-lah-reesh)* **dólares.**
Elas

(veer)
vir
to come

Eu _venho/_ _____ **do Brasil.**
                                                        from
                                                        (ee-tah-lee-ah)
Você _vem/_ _____ **da Itália.**
                                                        (kah-nah-dah)
Ele _____ **do Canadá.**
Ela
                                                        (een-glah-tair-hah)
Nós _vimos/_ _____ **da Inglaterra.**
                                                        England
                                                        (es-pahn-yah)
Eles _vêm/_ _____ **da Espanha.**
Elas   Spain

❐ **o metrô** *(meh-troh)*	subway	_____
❐ **metropolitano** *(meh-troh-poh-lee-tah-noo)*. . .	metropolitan	_____
❐ **o ministro** *(mee-nees-troo)*	minister (government)	_____
❐ **o minuto** *(mee-noo-too)*	minute	**m**
❐ **moderno** *(moh-dair-noo)*	modern	_____

Now take a break, walk around the room, take a deep breath **e** do the next *(saysh)* **seis** verbs.

(ehn-trar)
entrar
to enter

Eu _____ *(oh-tel)* **no hotel.**
into the

Você _____ **no banco.**

Ele _____ entra/ _____ *(hehs-tow-rahn-chee)* **no restaurante.**
Ela

Nós _____ **na casa.**

Eles _____ *(kwahr-too)* **no quarto.**
Elas
bedroom

(preh-see-zar) (dee)
precisar de
to need, to have need of

Eu _____ *(koh-poo) (ah-gwah)* **um copo de água.**
water
(sair-veh-zhah)
Você _____ precisa de/ _____ **uma cerveja.**
beer
(veen-yoo)
Ele _____ **um copo de vinho.**
Ela
wine
(doo-ahs) (shee-kah-rahs)
Nós _____ **duas xícaras de chá.**
two   cups   tea

Eles _____ **três xícaras de café.**
Elas

(ah-prehn-dair)
aprender
to learn

Eu _____ *(por-too-gaysh)* **português.**

Você _____ *(een-glaysh)* **inglês.**

Ele _____ *(ah-leh-mown)* **alemão.**
Ela
German
(frahn-saysh)
Nós _____ **francês.**
French
(shee-naysh)
Eles _____ aprendem/ _____ **chinês.**
Elas
Chinese

(vee-vair)
viver
to live

Eu _____ **nos Estados Unidos.**
(es-tah-doosh) (oo-nee-doosh)
in the   Unites States
(eh-oo-roh-pah)
Você _____ **na Europa.**
in

Ele _____ **no Canadá.**
Ela
in
(meh-shee-koo)
Nós _____ vivemos/ _____ **no México.**

Eles _____ **na Espanha.**
Elas

(vehn-dair)
vender
to sell

Eu _____ *(lee-vroosh)* **livros.**

Você _____ vende/ _____ *(kar-hoosh)* **carros.**
cars
(kar-toynsh) (pohs-tiesh)
Ele _____ **cartões postais.**
Ela
postcards

Nós _____ **ingressos.**

Eles _____ *(seh-loosh)* **selos.**
Elas
stamps

(heh-peh-cheer)
repetir
to repeat

Alô? Alô? Alô?

Eu _____ repito/ _____ **a palavra.**

Você _____ *(ehn-deh-reh-soo)* **o endereço.**
address

Ele _____ repete/ _____ **o nome.**
Ela
(jee-reh-soynsh)
Nós _____ repetimos/ _____ **as direções.**
directions
(nown)
Eles não _____ repetem/ _____ **nada.**
Elas
nothing

☐ **o momento** *(moh-mehn-too)* . . . . moment _____
☐ **o monastério** *(moh-nahs-teh-ree-oo)* . . . . monastery _____
☐ **a montanha** *(mohn-tahn-yah)* . . . . mountain **m** _____
☐ **o museu** *(moo-zeh-oo)* . . . . museum _____
☐ **a música** *(moo-zee-kah)* . . . . music _____

(seem)
Sim, it is hard to get used to all those **palavras novas.** Just keep practicing **e** before **você** know
yes   new

it, **você** will be using them naturally. **Agora** is a perfect time to turn to the back of this **livro,**

clip out your verb flash cards **e** start flashing. Don't skip over your free **palavras** either. Check

them off in the box provided as **você** *(ah-prehn-jee)* **aprende** each one. See if **você** can fill in the blanks below.
learn

(hehs-pohs-tahs)   *(pah-zhee-nah)*
As **respostas** are at the bottom of **a página.**
answers   page

1. _____

 (I speak Portuguese.)

2. _____

 (We learn Portuguese.)

3. _____

 (She needs ten reais.)

4. _____

 (He comes from Canada.)

5. _____

 (They live in the United States.)

6. _____

 (You buy a book.)

In the following Steps, **você** *(voh-say)* will be intro-

duced to more verbs **e você** should drill them

in exactly the same way as **você** did in this

section. Look up **as palavras novas** in your

(jee-see-oh-nah-ree-oo)
dicionário **e** make up your own sentences.
dictionary

Try out your **palavras novas** for that's how

you make them yours to use on your holiday.

Remember, the more **você** practice **agora,**

the more enjoyable your trip will be.

(boh-ah) (sor-chee)
Boa sorte!
good luck

(kay) (oh-rahs) (sown)
Que horas são?
what · time · is it

13

Você know how to tell **os dias** *(jee-ahs)* **da semana** *(seh-mah-nah)* **e os mêses** *(may-zeesh)* **do ano,** *(ah-noo)* so now let's learn to tell time.

As a traveler, **você** need to be able to tell time in order to make **reservas,** *(heh-zair-vahs)* **e** to catch **trens e** *(trains)*

(ow-nee-boos) **ônibus.** *(es-town)* **Aqui estão** the "basics." Keep in mind that the 24-hour clock system is frequently used.
buses · are

What time is it?	=	*(kay) (oh-rahs) (sown)* **Que horas são?** _____
	=	*(voh-say) (tame)* ~~**Você tem horas?**~~ _____ do you · have · the time
<u>minutes</u> AGORA	=	*(mee-noo-toosh)* **minutos** _____
half past	=	(the hour) + *(eh) (may-ah)* **e meia** _____
noon	=	*(may-oo-jee-ah)* **meio-dia** _____
midnight	=	*(may-ah-noy-chee)* **meia-noite** _____
a quarter	=	*(keen-zee)* **quinze** _____ 15 (minutes)
a quarter before	=	**quinze para às** *(ahs)* + (the hour) _____
a quarter after	=	(the hour) + **e quinze** _____

Agora quiz yourself. Fill in the missing letters below.

minutes = | m | | n | | t | | s | half past = | | ✕ | m | | | |

a quarter = | q | | | | | e | noon = | m | | o | - | | a |

midnight = | m | | a | - | | | e | and finally

What time is it? | Q | | ✕ | | o | | s | ✕ | ã | | ? |

☐ **a nação** *(nah-sown)*	nation	_____
☐ **natural** *(nah-too-rahl)*	natural	_____
☐ **naturalmente** *(nah-too-rahl-mehn-chee)*	naturally	**n** _____
☐ **não** *(nown)*	no, not	
☐ **náutico** *(now-chee-koo)*	nautical	

Agora, como are these **palavras** used? Study **os exemplos** *(eh-zame-ploosh)* **abaixo** *(ah-by-shoo)*. When **você** think it
_{how} _{examples} _{below}

through, it really is not too difficult. Just notice that the pattern changes after the halfway mark.

Notice that the phrase "o'clock" is not used.

(sown) *(oh-rahs)*
São cinco horas.   `5:00`   *São cinco horas. São cinco horas.*
_{it is}

(dehsh)
São cinco e dez.   `5:10`   _____

(keen-zee)
São cinco e quinze.   `5:15`   _____

(veen-chee)
São cinco e vinte.   `5:20`   _____

(may-ah)
São cinco e meia.   `5:30`   _____
_{half past five}

(saysh)
São vinte para às seis.   `5:40`   SAO CINCO Y QUARENTA
_{before}

São quinze para às seis.   `5:45`   SAO CINCO Y QUARENTA Y CINCO

São dez para às seis.   `5:50`   SAO CINCO Y CINQUENTA

São seis horas.   `6:00`   _____

(eem-por-tahn-chee) *(noo-meh-roosh)* *(pair-goon-tahs)*
See how **importante** **é** to learn **os números?** Answer the following **perguntas** based on the
_{it is} _{questions}
(heh-loh-zhee-oosh)
relógios below.
_{clocks}

1. `8:00`   _____

2. `7:15`   QUARTO (QUARTER OR RAH)

3. `4:30`   _____

4. `9:20`   _____

47

When **você** answer an "**A que horas?**" *(ah)(kay)(oh-rahs)* question, say "**às**" *(ahs)* before **você** give the time.

at what time   *at*

1.   **A que horas chega o trem?** *(ah)(kay)(oh-rahs)(sheh-gah)(trame)* _____ *às seis*
    at what time arrives train   (at 6:00)

2.   **A que horas chega o ônibus?** *(ow-nee-boos)* _____
      (at 7:30)

3.   **A que horas começa o concerto?** *(koh-meh-sah)(kohn-sair-too)* _____
    begins / commences   (at 20:00)

4.   **A que horas começa o filme?** *(feel-mee)* _____
    film   (at 21:00)

5.   **A que horas abre o restaurante?** *(ah-bree)(hehs-tow-rahn-chee)* _____
    opens   (at 11:30)

6.   **A que horas abre o banco?** _____
      (at 8:30)

7.   **A que horas fecha o restaurante?** *(feh-shah)(hehs-tow-rahn-chee)* _____
    closes   (at 2:00)

8.   **A que horas fecha o banco?** *(feh-shah)* _____
      (at 16:00)

Agora a quick quiz. Fill in the blanks **com** the correct **números**.

9. **Um minuto tem** _____ **segundos.** *(mee-noo-too)(tame)(seh-goon-doosh)*
   minute   (?)   seconds

10. **Uma hora tem** _____ **minutos.** *(mee-noo-toosh)*
   hour   (?)

11. **Uma semana tem** _____ **dias.** *(seh-mah-nah)(jee-ahs)*
   week   (?)

12. **Um ano tem** _____ **mêses.** *(ah-noo)(may-zeesh)*
   year   (?)   months

13. **Um ano tem** _____ **semanas.**
   (?)

14. **Um ano tem** _____ **dias.** *(jee-ahs)*
   (?)

AS RESPOSTAS

1. às seis
2. às sete e meia
3. às vinte
4. às vinte e uma
5. às onze e meia
6. às oito e meia
7. às duas horas
8. às dezesseis horas
9. sessenta
10. sessenta
11. sete
12. doze
13. cinqüenta e duas
14. trezentos e sessenta e cinco

Do **você** remember your greetings from earlier? It is a good time to review them as they will always be **muito** *(mwee-too)* **importante.** *(eem-por-tahn-chee)*
very

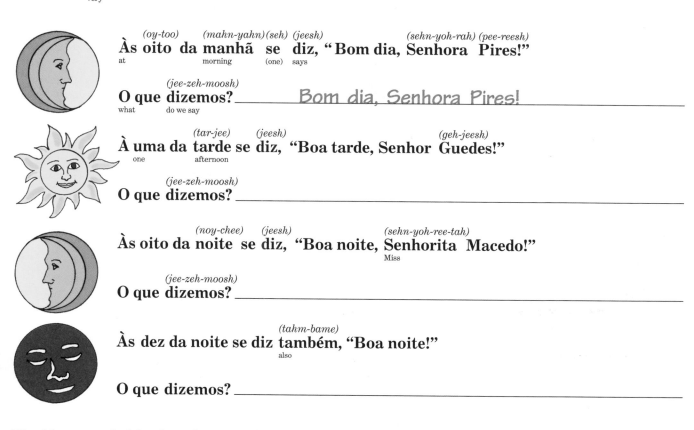

Às oito da manhã se diz, "Bom dia, Senhora Pires!"
(oy-too) *(mahn-yahn)* *(seh)* *(jeesh)* *(sehn-yoh-rah)* *(pee-reesh)*
at   morning   (one) says

O que dizemos? *(jee-zeh-moosh)* _____ Bom dia, Senhora Pires! _____
what   do we say

À uma da tarde se diz, "Boa tarde, Senhor Guedes!"
(tar-jee) *(jeesh)* *(geh-jeesh)*
one   afternoon

O que dizemos? *(jee-zeh-moosh)* _____

Às oito da noite se diz, "Boa noite, Senhorita Macedo!"
(noy-chee) *(jeesh)* *(sehn-yoh-ree-tah)*
Miss

O que dizemos? *(jee-zeh-moosh)* _____

Às dez da noite se diz também, "Boa noite!"
(tahm-bame)
also

O que dizemos? _____

Você have probably already noticed that plurals are *generally* formed by adding "s" after the final vowel.

a bicicleta *(ah) (bee-see-kleh-tah)*   **as bicicletas** *(ahs) (bee-see-kleh-tahs)*
bicycle
o telefone *(teh-leh-foh-nee)*   **os telefones** *(teh-leh-foh-neesh)*
o relógio *(heh-loh-zhee-oo)*   **os relógios** *(heh-loh-zhee-oosh)*
clock / watch

Em português adjectives agree with the gender and number of the nouns they modify **e** they generally come after the noun.

a bicicleta vermelha *(vair-mel-yah)*   **as bicicletas vermelhas** *(vair-mel-yahs)*
red
o telefone preto *(preh-too)*   **os telefones pretos** *(preh-toosh)*
black
o relógio novo *(heh-loh-zhee-oo) (noh-voo)*   **os relógios novos** *(noh-voosh)*
new

❏ **necessário** *(neh-sehs-sah-ree-oo)* . . . . necessary   _____
❏ **normal** *(nor-mahl)* . . . . normal   _____
❏ **o norte** *(nor-chee)* . . . . north   **O**   _____
❏ **november** *(noh-vem-bair)* . . . . November   _____
❏ **o número** *(noo-meh-roo)* . . . . number   _____

Aqui *(es-town)* **estão** the new verbs for Step 13.
are

(koh-mair)
comer _____
to eat

(beh-bair)
beber _____
to drink

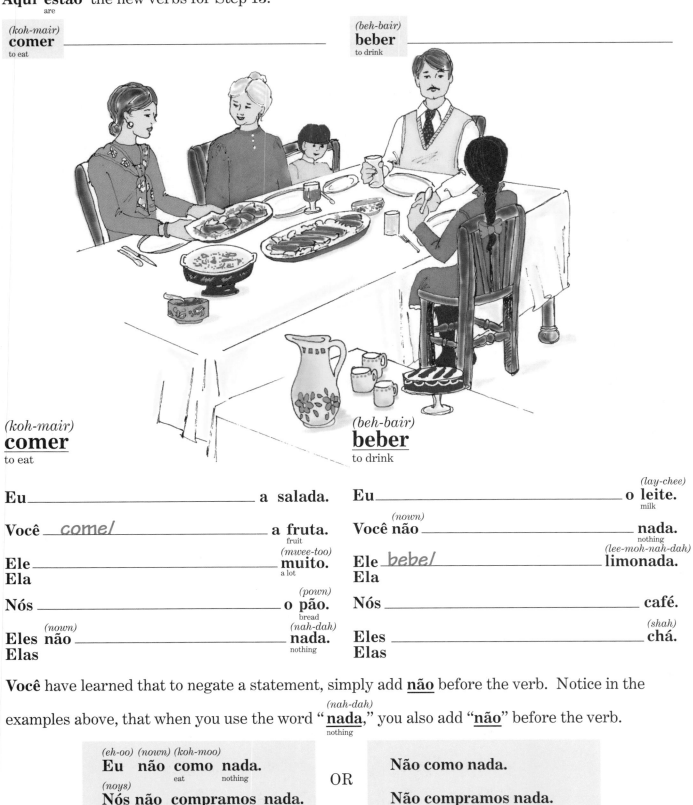

(koh-mair)
comer
to eat

(beh-bair)
beber
to drink

Eu _____ **a salada.**

Você _*comel*_____ **a fruta.**
fruit

Ele _____ *(mwee-too)* **muito.**
Ela   a lot

Nós _____ *(pown)* **o pão.**
bread

Eles *(nown)* **não** _____ *(nah-dah)* **nada.**
Elas   nothing

Eu _____ *(lay-chee)* **o leite.**
milk

Você não _*(nown)*_____ **nada.**
nothing

Ele _*bebel*_____ *(lee-moh-nah-dah)* **limonada.**
Ela

Nós _____ **café.**

Eles _____ *(shah)* **chá.**
Elas

Você have learned that to negate a statement, simply add **não** before the verb. Notice in the

examples above, that when you use the word " *(nah-dah)* **nada**," you also add "**não**" before the verb.
nothing

(eh-oo) *(nown)* *(koh-moo)* **Eu não como nada.**		
eat nothing	OR	**Não como nada.**
(noys) **Nós não compramos nada.** we buy nothing		**Não compramos nada.**

❑ **o objeto** *(ohb-zheh-too)* . . . . object _____
❑ **a ocasião** *(oh-kah-zee-own)* . . . . occasion _____
❑ **o oceano** *(oh-seh-ah-noo)* . . . . ocean **o** _____
❑ **o ocidente** *(oh-see-dehn-chee)* . . . . occident, west _____
❑ **ocupado** *(oh-koo-pah-doo)* . . . . occupied _____

50

(voh-say)

Você have learned a lot of material in the last few steps **e** that means it is time to quiz yourself.

Don't panic, this is just for you **e** no one else needs to know how **você** did. Remember, this is a chance to review, find out what **você** remember **e** what **você** need to spend more time on.

(hehs-pohs-tahs)

After **você** have finished, check your **respostas** in the glossary at the back of this book.

Circle the correct answers.

café -	tea	coffee	**família -**	seven	family
sim -	yes	no	**filhos -**	children	grandfather
tia -	aunt	uncle	**leite -**	butter	(milk)
ou -	and	or	**sal -**	pepper	salt
aprender -	to drink	to learn	**embaixo de -**	under	over
noite -	morning	night	**homem -**	man	doctor
terça-feira -	Friday	Tuesday	**junho -**	June	July
falar -	to live	to speak	**cozinha -**	kitchen	religion
verão -	summer	winter	**tenho -**	I want	I have
dinheiro -	money	page	**comprar -**	to order	to buy
dez -	nine	ten	**ontem -**	yesterday	tomorrow
muito -	a lot	bread	**bom -**	good	yellow

Como vai? *(vy)*   <u>What time is it?</u>   <u>How are you?</u>   Well, how are you after this quiz?

❐ **a ópera** *(oh-peh-rah)* . . . . opera
❐ **a operação** *(oh-peh-rah-sown)* . . . . operation
❐ **a opção** *(ohp-sown)* . . . . option   **o**
❐ **a oportunidade** *(oh-por-too-nee-dah-jee)* . . . . . opportunity
❐ **a oposição** *(oh-poh-zee-sown)* . . . . opposition

_____
_____
_____
_____
_____

14

(nor-chee) *(sool)* *(lehs-chee)* *(oh-ehs-chee)*
Norte - Sul, Leste - Oeste
north   south   east   west

If **você** are looking at **um mapa** *(mah-pah)* **e você** see the following **palavras,** it should not be too difficult
map
to figure out what they mean. Take an educated guess.

(ah-meh-ree-kah) (doo) (nor-chee)   *(sool)*
América do Norte   **América do Sul**

(poh-loo)
Pólo Norte   **Pólo Sul**

(kohs-tah) (lehs-chee)   *(oh-ehs-chee)*
a costa do leste   **a costa do oeste**

(eer-lahn-dah)   *(ah-free-kah)*
Irlanda do Norte   **África do Sul**

(por-too-gay-zahs)
As palavras portuguesas "north," "south," "east," **e** "west" are easy to recognize due to

their similarity to **inglês**. These **palavras são muito importantes**. Learn them **hoje!**
(sown) (mwee-too) (eem-por-tahn-chees)   *(oh-zhee)*
are

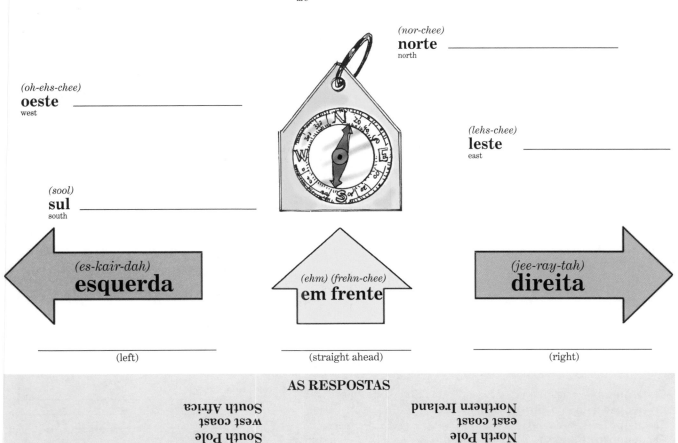

(nor-chee)
norte _____
north

(oh-ehs-chee)
oeste _____
west

(lehs-chee)
leste _____
east

(sool)
sul _____
south

(es-kair-dah)
esquerda

(ehm) (frehn-chee)
em frente

(jee-ray-tah)
direita

_____   _____   _____
(left)   (straight ahead)   (right)

AS RESPOSTAS

South Africa   Northern Ireland
west coast   east coast
South Pole   North Pole
South America   North America

These **palavras** can go a long way. Say them aloud each time you write them in the blanks below.

(por) (fah-vor)
por favor _____
please / excuse me (to catch attention)

(kohm) (lee-sehn-sah)
com licença _____
excuse me (when interrupting)

(dehs-kool-pee)
desculpe _____
excuse me (as in I am sorry)

(oh-bree-gah-doo) (oh-bree-gah-dah)
obrigado / obrigada _____
thank you (♂)　　thank you (♀)

(jee) (nah-dah)
de nada _____
you're welcome

(doo-ahs) (kohn-vair-sah-soynsh) *(chee-pee-kahs)*
Aqui estão duas conversações very **típicas** **para** someone who is trying to find something.
　　　　　two　　conversations　　　　typical　　for

Write them out in the blanks below.

João:
(oh-tel) (koh-pah-kah-bah-nah) (pah-lah-see)
Por favor. Onde é o Hotel Copacabana Palace?

_____ *Por favor. Onde é o Hotel Copacabana Palace?* _____

Carlos:
(vy)　　　　(vee-ree)
Vai em frente e vire na segunda à esquerda.
　go　straight ahead　　turn　　second　　　left

_____

(pah-lah-see)　　(jee-ray-tah)
O Hotel Copacabana Palace é à direita.

_____

Orlando:
(moo-zeh-oo)　(ar-chees)
Por favor. Onde é o Museu de Artes?

_____

Cristina:
(vee-ree) (jee-ray-tah) (vy)　　　　(ah-proh-see-mah-dah-mehn-chee) (same) (meh-troosh)
Vire à direita e vai em frente aproximadamente cem metros.
　turn　　　　　　go　　　　　approximately　　　　　　meters

_____

O Museu de Artes é à esquerda.

_____

❐ **ordinário** *(or-jee-nah-ree-oo)* . . . . ordinary
❐ **oriental** *(oh-ree-ehn-tahl)* . . . . oriental
❐ **original** *(oh-ree-zhee-nahl)* . . . . original　　**O**
❐ **a ostra** *(ohs-trah)* . . . . oyster
❐ **oval** *(oh-vahl)* . . . . oval

_____
_____
_____
_____

Are **você** lost? There is no need to be lost if **você** have learned the basic direction **palavras**.

(kohn-vair-sah-soynsh)
Do not try to memorize these **conversações** because **você** will never be looking for precisely

(jee-reh-soynsh)   *(hee-oo)* *(pah-lah-see)*
these places. One day, **você** might need to ask **direções** to "**O Hotel Rio Palace**" or
directions

(hehs-tow-rahn-chee) *(kah-roh-lee-nee)*
"**Restaurante Caroline**." Learn the key direction **palavras e** be sure **você** can find your

destination. **Você** may want to buy a guidebook to start planning which places **você** would like

(jee-reh-soynsh)
to visit. Practice asking **direções** to these special places. What if the person responding to

(pair-goon-tah)
your **pergunta** answers too quickly for **você** to understand the entire reply? Practice saying,
question

(dehs-kool-pee)   *(nown)* *(ehn-tehn-doo)*   *(poh-jee)* *(heh-peh-cheer)*
Desculpe.   Não entendo.   Pode repetir,   por favor?
I do not understand   can you   repeat

Agora, say it again **e** then write it out below.

_____
(Excuse me. I do not understand. Can you repeat, please?)

(seem)   *(jee-fee-seel)*
Sim, é difícil at first but don't give up! **Quando** the directions are repeated, **você** will be able to
yes   it is difficult   when

understand if **você** have learned the key **palavras**. Let's review by writing them in the blanks below.

right

left

_____
(north)

_____ (west)

_____ (east)

_____
(south)

☐ **o palácio** *(pah-lah-see-oo)*	palace	
☐ **a palma** *(pahl-mah)*	palm	
☐ **o pânico** *(pah-nee-koo)*	panic	**p**
☐ **o passaporte** *(pahs-sah-por-chee)*	passport	
☐ **a pausa** *(pow-zah)*	pause	

(es-town) *(noh-voosh)*

Aqui estão quatro verbs **novos.**
are · new

(ehn-kohn-trar)
encontrar _____
to find, to meet

(mahn-dar)
mandar _____
to send

(ehn-tehn-dair)
entender _____
to understand

(es-kreh-vair)
escrever _____
to write

As always, say each sentence out loud. Say each **e** every **palavra** carefully, pronouncing each

(por-too-gaysh)
sound **em português** as well as **você** can.

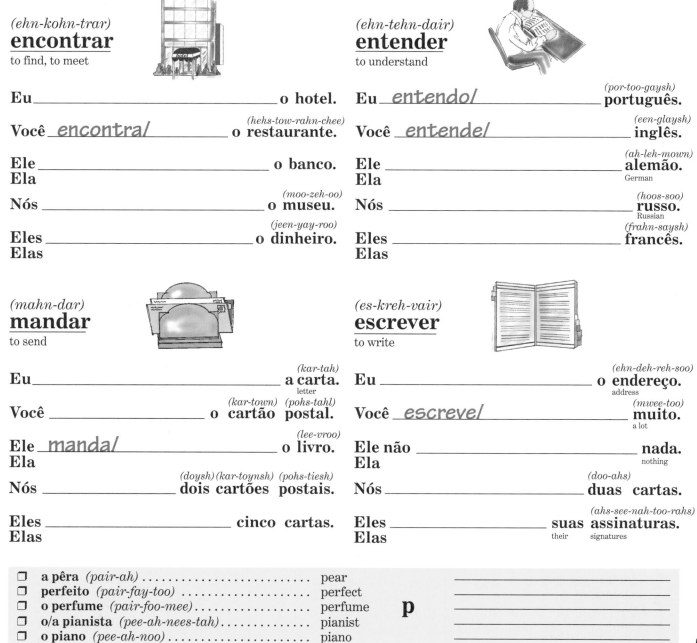

(ehn-kohn-trar)
encontrar
to find, to meet

Eu _____ o hotel.

(hehs-tow-rahn-chee)
Você _encontra/_ _____ o restaurante.

Ele _____ o banco.
Ela

(moo-zeh-oo)
Nós _____ o museu.

(jeen-yay-roo)
Eles _____ o dinheiro.
Elas

(ehn-tehn-dair)
entender
to understand

(por-too-gaysh)
Eu _entendo/_ _____ português.

(een-glaysh)
Você _entende/_ _____ inglês.

(ah-leh-mown)
Ele _____ alemão.
Ela · German

(hoos-soo)
Nós _____ russo.
· Russian
(frahn-saysh)
Eles _____ francês.
Elas

(mahn-dar)
mandar
to send

(kar-tah)
Eu _____ a carta.
· letter
(kar-town) *(pohs-tahl)*
Você _____ o cartão postal.

(lee-vroo)
Ele _manda/_ _____ o livro.
Ela

(doysh)(kar-toynsh)(pohs-tiesh)
Nós _____ dois cartões postais.

Eles _____ cinco cartas.
Elas

(es-kreh-vair)
escrever
to write

(ehn-deh-reh-soo)
Eu _____ o endereço.
· address
(mwee-too)
Você _escreve/_ _____ muito.
· a lot
Ele não _____ nada.
Ela · nothing
(doo-ahs)
Nós _____ duas cartas.

(ahs-see-nah-too-rahs)
Eles _____ suas assinaturas.
Elas · their · signatures

❐ **a pêra** *(pair-ah)* .... pear
❐ **perfeito** *(pair-fay-too)* .... perfect
❐ **o perfume** *(pair-foo-mee)* .... perfume **p**
❐ **o/a pianista** *(pee-ah-nees-tah)* .... pianist
❐ **o piano** *(pee-ah-noo)* .... piano

_____
_____
_____
_____

15   *(ehm) (see-mah) (ehm-by-shoo)*
Em cima – Embaixo
upstairs   downstairs

Aqui *(noys)* **nós** *(ah-prehn-deh-moosh)* **aprendemos** *(mysh)* **mais palavras.** Imagine that this **é uma casa em São Paulo.** *(sown) (pow-loo)*

learn   more

Go to your **quarto e** *(kwahr-too)* look around **o quarto.** Let's learn the names of the things **no seu** *(seh-oo)* **quarto,**

in   your

just like **nós** *(noys)* learned the various parts of **a casa.**

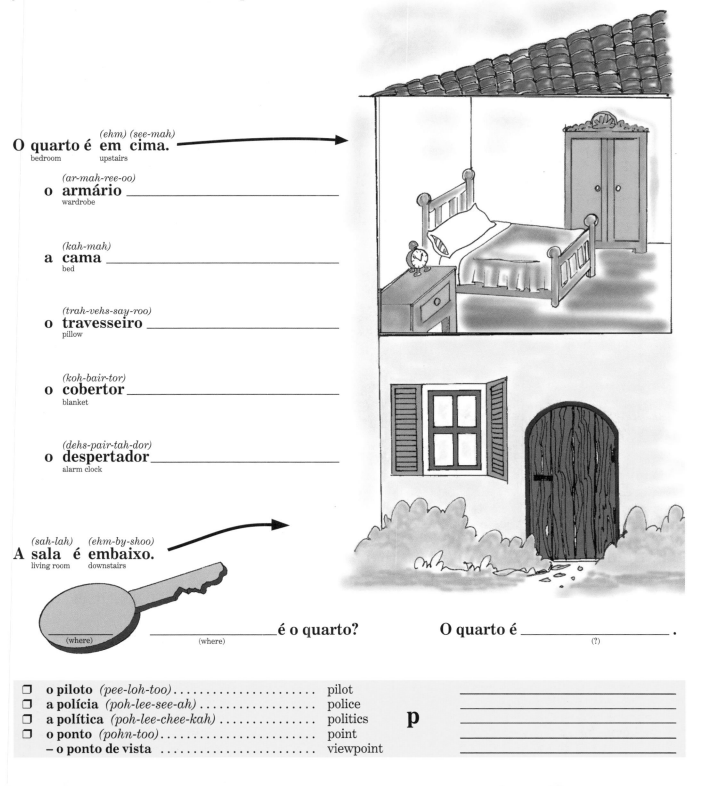

O quarto é em cima. *(ehm) (see-mah)*
bedroom   upstairs

o **armário** _____ *(ar-mah-ree-oo)*
wardrobe

a **cama** _____ *(kah-mah)*
bed

o **travesseiro** _____ *(trah-vehs-say-roo)*
pillow

o **cobertor** _____ *(koh-bair-tor)*
blanket

o **despertador** _____ *(dehs-pair-tah-dor)*
alarm clock

A sala é embaixo. *(sah-lah) (ehm-by-shoo)*
living room   downstairs

_____ (where)

_____ é o quarto?   **O quarto é** _____ .
(where)   (?)

❏ **o piloto** *(pee-loh-too)*	pilot	_____
❏ **a polícia** *(poh-lee-see-ah)*	police	_____
❏ **a política** *(poh-lee-chee-kah)*	politics **p**	_____
❏ **o ponto** *(pohn-too)*	point	_____
– **o ponto de vista**	viewpoint	_____

Agora, remove the next **cinco** stickers **e** label these things **no seu** *(seh-oo)* **quarto.** Let's move **para o**
your   *to*   *the*

(bahn-yay-roo)
banheiro e do the same thing. Restrooms may be marked with pictures **ou** simply with the

letters **D** **ou** **C.** **Você** may also see the women's restroom labeled **"Damas"** *(dah-mahs)* **ou** **"Mulheres."** *(mool-yair-eesh)*

(kah-vahl-yay-roosh)   *(oh-mehns)*
Either **"Cavalheiros" ou "Homens"** is used to identify the men's restroom.

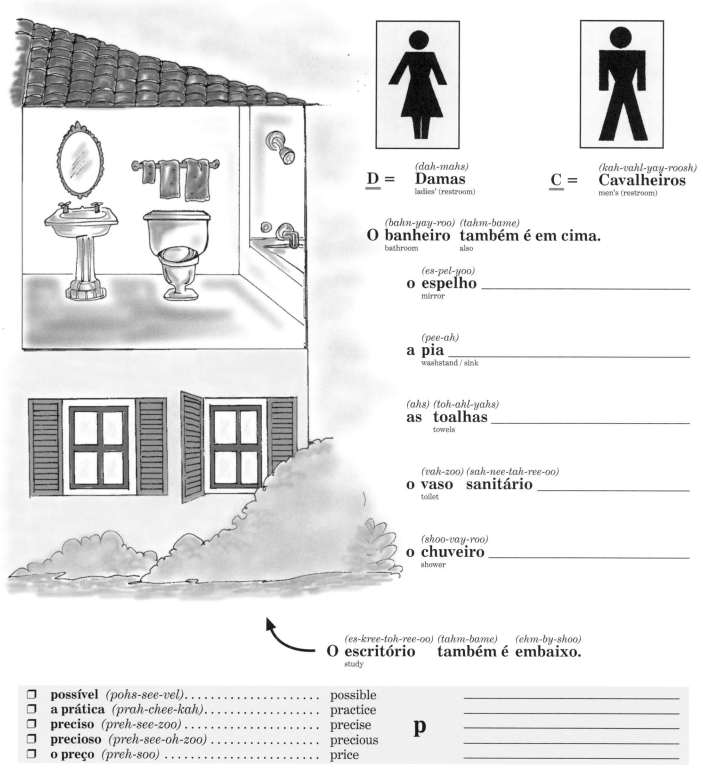

D =	*(dah-mahs)* **Damas** ladies' (restroom)	**C =**	*(kah-vahl-yay-roosh)* **Cavalheiros** men's (restroom)

(bahn-yay-roo) (tahm-bame)
O banheiro também é em cima.
bathroom   also

(es-pel-yoo)
o espelho _____
mirror

(pee-ah)
a pia _____
washstand / sink

(ahs) (toh-ahl-yahs)
as toalhas _____
towels

(vah-zoo) (sah-nee-tah-ree-oo)
o vaso   sanitário _____
toilet

(shoo-vay-roo)
o chuveiro _____
shower

(es-kree-toh-ree-oo) (tahm-bame)   (ehm-by-shoo)
O escritório   também é embaixo.
study

❐ **possível** *(pohs-see-vel)*	possible	_____
❐ **a prática** *(prah-chee-kah)*	practice	_____
❐ **preciso** *(preh-see-zoo)*	precise	_____
❐ **precioso** *(preh-see-oh-zoo)*	precious	_____
❐ **o preço** *(preh-soo)*	price	_____

p

Não *(noun)* forget to remove the next group of stickers **e** label these things in your **banheiro.** Okay, it is time to review. Here's a quick quiz to see what you remember.

men's (restroom)

I understand

downstairs

please

towels

upstairs

bathroom / restroom

to repeat

straight ahead

women's (restroom)

(ehm-by-shoo)
embaixo

(kah-vahl-yay-roosh)
cavalheiros

por favor

(ehn-tehn-doo)
eu entendo

(heh-peh-cheer)
repetir

(frehn-chee)
em frente

damas

(toh-ahl-yahs)
as toalhas

em cima

(bahn-yay-roo)
o banheiro

❑ **o presente** *(preh-zehn-chee)*	present, gift	
❑ **principal** *(preen-see-pahl)*	principal, main	
❑ **o problema** *(proh-bleh-mah)*	problem	**p**
❑ **o produto** *(proh-doo-too)*	product	
❑ **o professor** *(proh-fehs-sor)*	professor	

Next stop — **o escritório,** *(es-kree-toh-ree-oo)* specifically **a mesa do escritório.** *(meh-zah)* *(es-kree-toh-ree-oo)* **O que está sobre a mesa?** *(kay)* *(soh-bree)*

office — table / desk — on

Let's identify **as coisas** *(koy-zahs)* which one normally finds **sobre a mesa** or strewn about **o escritório.**

things

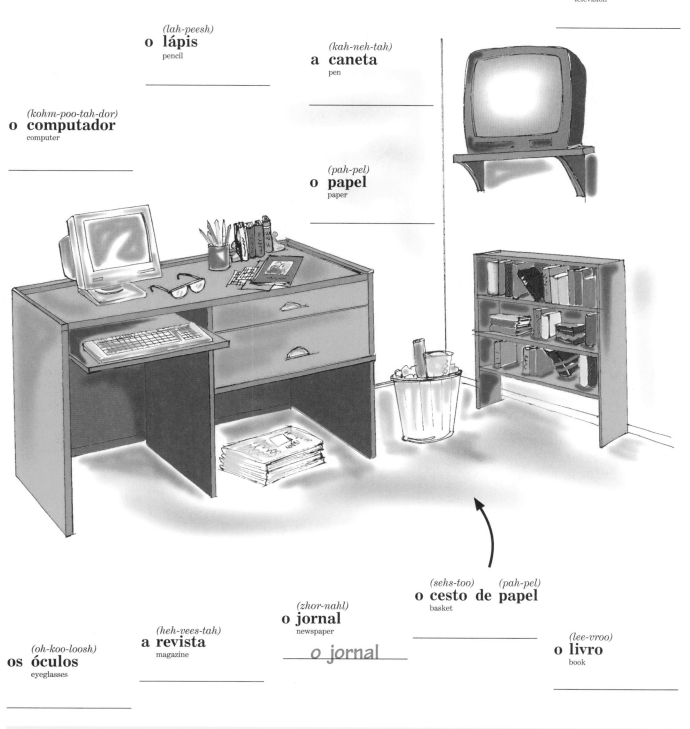

(lah-peesh)
o lápis
pencil

(kah-neh-tah)
a caneta
pen

(teh-leh-vee-zown)
a televisão
television

(kohm-poo-tah-dor)
o computador
computer

(pah-pel)
o papel
paper

(sehs-too) *(pah-pel)*
o cesto de papel
basket

(zhor-nahl)
o jornal
newspaper

o jornal

(heh-vees-tah)
a revista
magazine

(oh-koo-loosh)
os óculos
eyeglasses

(lee-vroo)
o livro
book

☐ **o programa** *(proh-grah-mah)*	program	
☐ **proibido** *(proh-ee-bee-doo)*	prohibited, forbidden	
☐ **a promessa** *(proh-mehs-sah)*	promise	**p**
☐ **a pronúncia** *(proh-noon-see-ah)*	pronunciation	
☐ **o público** *(poo-blee-koo)*	public	

Don't forget these essentials!

(kar-tah)
a carta
letter

(seh-loo)
o selo
stamp

(kar-town) (pohs-tahl)
o cartão postal
postcard

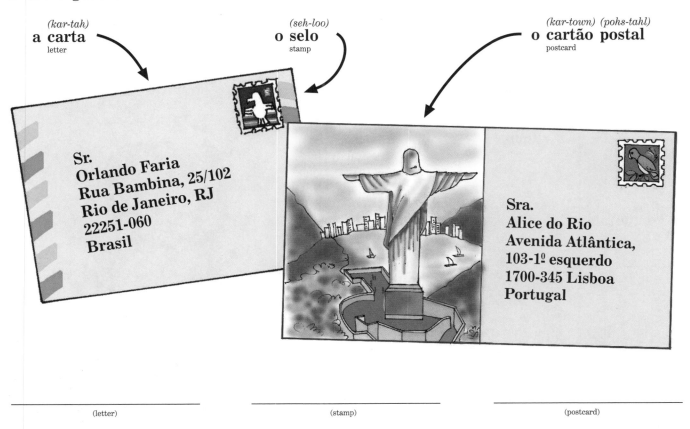

Sr.
Orlando Faria
Rua Bambina, 25/102
Rio de Janeiro, RJ
22251-060
Brasil

Sra.
Alice do Rio
Avenida Atlântica,
103-1º esquerdo
1700-345 Lisboa
Portugal

_____   _____   _____
(letter)   (stamp)   (postcard)

(kar-nah-vahl)
Carnaval no Brasil é a party celebrated by the entire country. The dates vary from **ano** to **ano,**

but officially **Carnaval** starts **no sábado** before **e** finishes on Ash Wednesday. The parade of the

(es-koh-lahs)   *(sahm-bah)*
Escolas de Samba é "the event" with thousands of people wearing glamorous costumes **e**
schools

dancing enthusiastically while competing for Brazil's "World Cup of **Carnaval.**"

Remember if you add **<u>não</u>** before a verb **você** negate the sentence.
not

(kair-oo)   *(koh-poo)*
Eu quero um copo de água.
want   glass   water

Eu não quero um copo de água.
do not want

Em português, you may drop the subject of the sentence as long as the meaning remains clear.

Eu entendo português.
understand

Nós vimos dos Estados Unidos.
come

OR

Entendo português.

Vimos dos Estados Unidos.

❏	**o rádio** *(hah-joo)*	radio		_____
❏	**a raça** *(hah-sah)*	race		_____
❏	**o raio** *(hi-oo)*	ray	**r**	_____
❏	**rápido** *(hah-pee-doo)*	rapid		_____
❏	**a reação** *(heh-ah-sown)*	reaction		_____

Simple, isn't it? **Agora**, after you fill in the blanks below, go back a second time and negate all these sentences by adding "**não**" _(nown)_ before each verb. Then go back a third time **e** drop the subject. **Você** will see some verbs which do not conform to the patterns. Don't get discouraged! Just look at how much **você** have already learned **e** think ahead to beautiful **praias**, _(pry-ahs)_ beaches **Pão de** _(pown)_ _(jeh)_ Sugar Loaf

(ah-soo-kar)
Açúcar, **e** new adventures **no Rio**.

(teh-leh-foh-nar)
telefonar _____
to phone, to call

(dor-meer)
dormir _____
to sleep

(pah-gar)
pagar _____
to pay, to pay for

(mee) (dah) _(por)_ _(fah-vor)_
me dá . . . por favor _____
give me   please

(teh-leh-foh-nar)
telefonar
to phone, to call

Eu _____ **para o Canadá.**
                                                    to

Você _____ **para os Estados Unidos.**

Ele _telefona/_ _____ **para a Itália.**
Ela

Nós _____ **para a Inglaterra.**

Eles _____ **à cobrar.** _(koh-brar)_ collect
Elas

(pah-gar)
pagar
to pay, to pay for

Eu _pago/_ _____ **a conta.** _(kohn-tah)_ bill

Você _____ **os ingressos do teatro.** _(een-grehs-soos)_ tickets _(teh-ah-troo)_ theater

Ele _____ **os ingressos do balé.** _(bah-lay)_ ballet
Ela

Nós _____ **os ingressos do museu.** _(moo-zeh-oo)_

Eles _____ **os ingressos do concerto.** _(kohn-sair-too)_ concert
Elas

(dor-meer)
dormir
to sleep

Eu _durmo/_ _____ **no quarto.** _(kwahr-too)_ bedroom

Você _dorme/_ _____ **no hotel.**

Ele _____ **na casa.**
Ela

Nós _dormimos/_ **embaixo do cobertor.** _(ehm-by-shoo)_ under _(koh-bair-tor)_ blanket

Eles _dormem/_ **sem os travesseiros.** _(same)_ without _(trah-vehs-say-roosh)_ pillows
Elas

(mee) (dah) _(fah-vor)_
me dá . . . por favor
give me   please

_Me dá/_ _____ **a conta,** _por favor/_ . _(kohn-tah)_ bill

_____ **o menu,** _____ . _(meh-noo)_

_____ **o ingresso,** _____ . _(een-grehs-soo)_

_____ **o endereço,** _____ . _(ehn-deh-reh-soo)_ address

_____ **o nome,** _____ .

❏ **a rebelião** _(heh-beh-lee-own)_	rebellion		_____
❏ **receber** _(heh-seh-bair)_	to receive		_____
❏ **regular** _(heh-goo-lar)_	regular	**r**	_____
❏ **a relação** _(heh-lah-sown)_	relation		_____
❏ **a religião** _(heh-lee-zhee-own)_	religion		_____

Before **você** proceed with the next step, **por favor** identify all the items **abaixo.**
(ah-by-shoo)
below

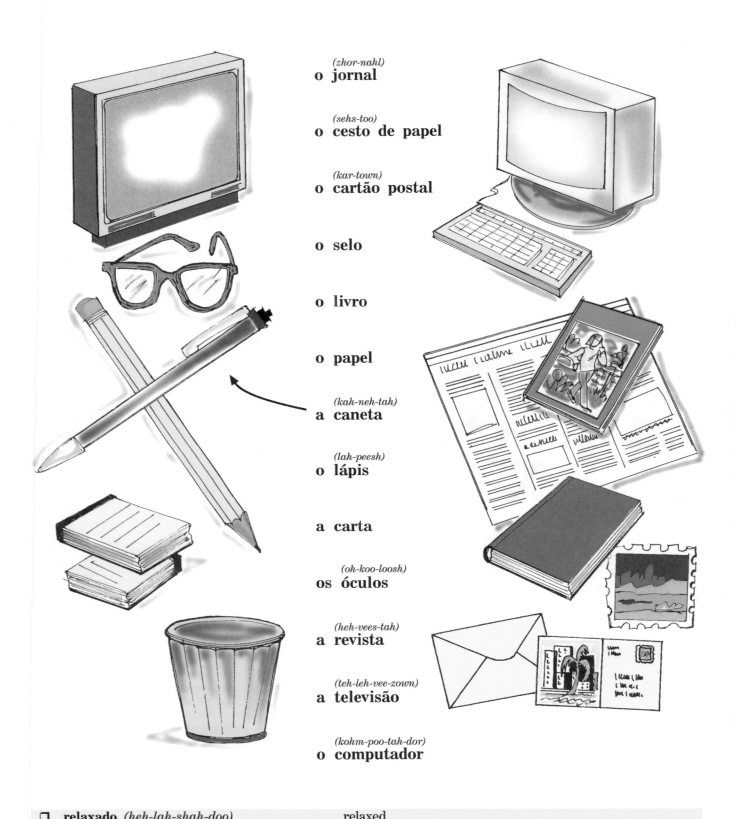

(zhor-nahl)
o **jornal**

(sehs-too)
o **cesto de papel**

(kar-town)
o **cartão postal**

o **selo**

o **livro**

o **papel**

(kah-neh-tah)
a **caneta**

(lah-peesh)
o **lápis**

a **carta**

(oh-koo-loosh)
os **óculos**

(heh-vees-tah)
a **revista**

(teh-leh-vee-zown)
a **televisão**

(kohm-poo-tah-dor)
o **computador**

❏	**relaxado** *(heh-lah-shah-doo)*	relaxed
❏	**repetir** *(heh-peh-cheer)*	to repeat
	– Repita por favor!	Please repeat! **r**
❏	**a república** *(heh-poo-blee-kah)*	republic
❏	**a reserva** *(heh-zair-vah)*	reservation

16

(kor-hay-oo)
O Correio
mail / post office

Agora você know how to count, how to ask *(pair-goon-tahs)* **perguntas,** how to use verbs **com** the "plug-in"
questions

formula **e** how to describe something, be it the location of **um hotel ou a cor de uma casa.** Let's
color

take the basics that **você** have learned **e** expand them in special areas that will be most helpful

in your travels. What does everyone do on a vacation? Send **cartões** *(kar-toynsh)* **postais,** *(pohs-tiesh)* of course! Let's

learn exactly how **a agência** *(ah-zhayn-see-ah)* **do correio,** *(kor-hay-oo)* or simply **"correio"** *(kor-hay-oo)* works.
the post office

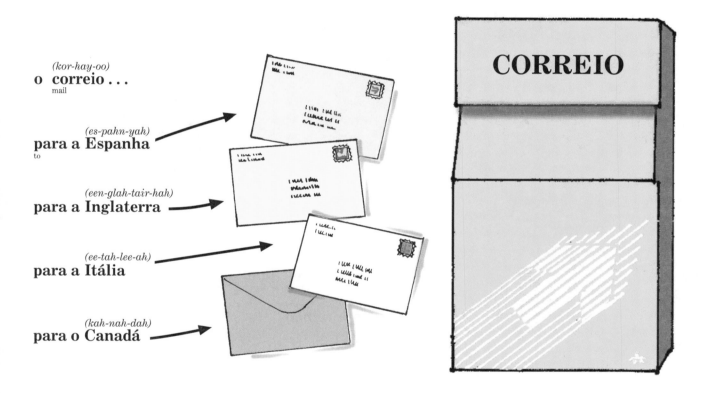

(kor-hay-oo)
o correio . . .
mail

(es-pahn-yah)
para a Espanha
to

(een-glah-tair-hah)
para a Inglaterra

(ee-tah-lee-ah)
para a Itália

(kah-nah-dah)
para o Canadá

CORREIO

(kor-hay-oo)
O correio is where **você** buy **selos,** *(seh-loosh)* send **pacotes,** *(pah-koh-chees)* **cartas e cartões** *(kar-toynsh)* **postais.** *(pohs-tiesh)* In large cities,
post office   packages

você can send **um fax** *(fahks)* **ou e-mail** *(ee-may-oo)* **do correio. No correio você** can also buy **um cartão de** *(kar-town)*
phone card

telefone *(teh-leh-foh-nee)* **e** make **cópias.** *(koh-pee-ahs)*
copies

❑ **o restaurante** *(hehs-tow-rahn-chee)*	restautant		_____
❑ **a revolução** *(heh-voh-loo-sown)*	revolution		_____
❑ **romano** *(hoh-mah-noo)*	Roman	**r**	_____
❑ **romântico** *(hoh-mahn-chee-koo)*	romantic		_____
❑ **o rubi** *(hoo-bee)*	ruby		_____

Aqui estão the necessary **palavras para o correio.** Practice them aloud **e** write them in the blanks.

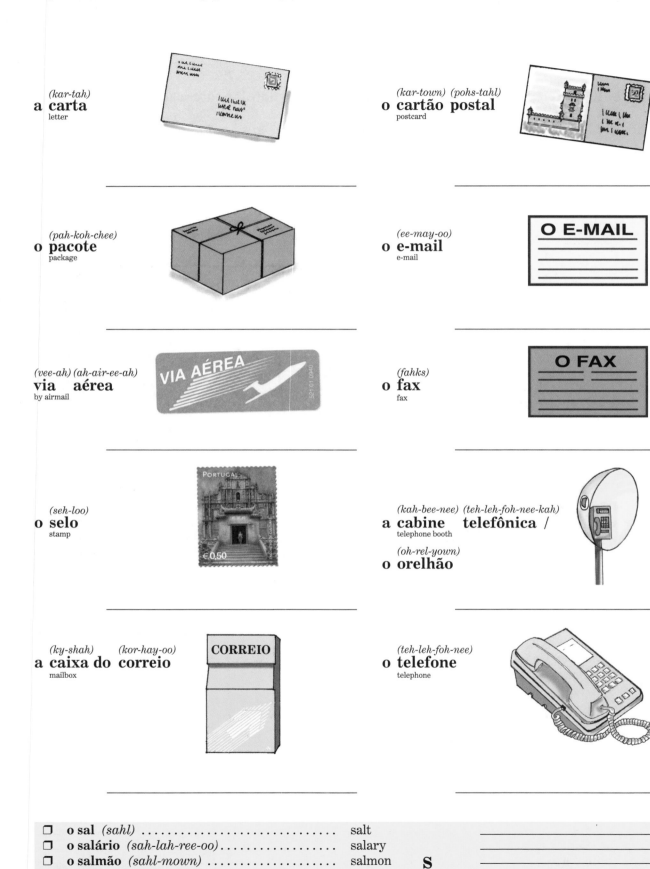

(kar-tah)
a carta
letter

(kar-town) (pohs-tahl)
o cartão postal
postcard

_____

(pah-koh-chee)
o pacote
package

(ee-may-oo)
o e-mail
e-mail

O E-MAIL

_____

(vee-ah) (ah-air-ee-ah)
via aérea
by airmail

VIA AÉREA

(fahks)
o fax
fax

O FAX

_____

(seh-loo)
o selo
stamp

(kah-bee-nee) (teh-leh-foh-nee-kah)
a cabine telefônica /
telephone booth

(oh-rel-yown)
o orelhão

_____

(ky-shah) (kor-hay-oo)
a caixa do correio
mailbox

CORREIO

(teh-leh-foh-nee)
o telefone
telephone

_____

❑ **o sal** *(sahl)*	salt	_____
❑ **o salário** *(sah-lah-ree-oo)*	salary	_____
❑ **o salmão** *(sahl-mown)*	salmon **S**	_____
❑ **o santo** *(sahn-too)*	saint	_____
❑ **a sardinha** *(sar-jeen-yah)*	sardine	_____

64

Next step — **você** ask **perguntas** *(pair-goon-tahs)* like those **abaixo,** *(ah-by-shoo)* depending on what **você quer.** *(kair)* Repeat these sentences aloud many times.

(ohn-jee) (kohm-proo) (seh-loosh)
Onde compro selos? _____
do I buy

(kar-town)
Onde compro um cartão postal? _____

(ah) *(teh-leh-foh-nee)*
Onde há um telefone? _____
is there

(ah) *(ky-shah)* *(kor-hay-oo)*
Onde há uma caixa do correio? _____
is there   mailbox

Onde há uma cabine telefônica? _____
telephone booth

(pohs-soo)(mahn-dar) *(pah-koh-chee)*
Onde posso mandar um pacote? _____
can I   send

(fah-zair) *(shah-mah-dah) (loh-kahl)*
Onde posso fazer uma chamada local? _____
can I   make   call

Quanto custa isso? _____ *Quanto custa isso? Quanto custa isso?* _____

Agora, quiz yourself. See if **você** can translate the following thoughts into **português.**

1.   Where is there a telephone booth? _____

2.   Where can I phone to the U.S.A.? _____

3.   Where can I make a local telephone call? _____

4.   Where is the post office? _____

5.   Where can I buy stamps? _____

6.   Airmail stamps? _____

7.   Where can I send a package? _____

8.   Where can I send a fax? _____

Aqui estão mais verbos.
(mysh) more *(vair-boosh)* verbs

(fah-zair)
fazer _____
to make, to do

(vair)
ver _____
to see

(jee-zair)
dizer _____
to say

(eer)
ir _____
to go

Practice these verbs by not only filling in the blanks, but by saying them aloud many, many

times until you are comfortable with the sounds **e** the words.

(fah-zair)
fazer
to make, to do

Eu _faço/_ _____ **tudo.** *(too-doo)* everything

Você não _faz/_ _____ **nada.** nothing

Ele não _____ **muito.** *(mwee-too)*
Ela

Nós não _fazemos/_ _____ **a cama.**

Eles _fazem/_ _____ **o café.**
Elas

(jee-zair)
dizer
to say

Oi!

Eu _digo/_ _____ **"oi."** *(oy)* hi

Você _diz/_ _____ **"sim."**

Ele _____ **"não."**
Ela

Nós _dizemos/_ _____ **"tchau" ou "adeus."** *(chow)* *(ah-deh-oos)*

Eles não _dizem/_ _____ **nada.**
Elas

(vair)
ver
to see

Eu _vejo/_ _____ **o mercado.** *(mair-kah-doo)* market

Você _vê/_ _____ **o Museu de Artes.** *(ar-chees)*

Ele _____ **o Teatro Municipal.** *(moo-nee-see-pahl)*
Ela — Municipal Theater

Nós _vemos/_ **o Oceano Atlântico.** *(oh-seh-ah-noo)* *(aht-lahn-chee-koo)*
Ocean — Atlantic

Eles _vêem/_ _____ **as montanhas.** *(mohn-tahn-yahs)*
Elas — mountains

(eer)
ir
to go

Eu _vou/_ _____ **à praia.** *(pry-ah)* beach

Você _vai/_ _____ **ao concerto.** *(ah-oh)*

Ele _vai/_ _____ **ao hotel.**
Ela

Nós _vamos/_ _____ **à cidade.** *(see-dah-jee)* city

Eles _vão/_ _____ **à igreja.** *(ee-greh-zhah)* church
Elas

☐ **a secretária** *(seh-kreh-tah-ree-ah)* . . . . secretary (♀)
☐ **o secretário** *(seh-kreh-tah-ree-oo)* . . . . secretary (♂)
☐ **a seleção** *(seh-leh-sown)* . . . . selection **s** _____
☐ **a sensação** *(sehn-sah-sown)* . . . . sensation
☐ **o serviço** *(sair-vee-soo)* . . . . service

Some of these signs you probably recognize, but take a couple of minutes to review them anyway.

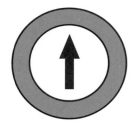

(see-gah)　*(frehn-chee)*
siga em frente
go　straight ahead

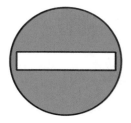

(ahl-fane-deh-gah)
alfândega
customs

(ehn-trah-dah) (proh-ee-bee-dah)
entrada proibida
no entrance

(ah-air-oh-por-too)
aeroporto
airport

(proh-ee-bee-doo) (vee-rar) (es-kair-dah)
proibido virar à esquerda
no left turn

(veh-loh-see-dah-jee) (mah-see-mah)
velocidade máxima
speed limit

(proh-ee-bee-doo)(es-tah-see-oh-nar)
proibido estacionar
no parking

(proh-ee-bee-doo) (ool-trah-pahs-sar)
proibido ultrapassar
no passing

(pah-ree)
pare
stop

(dehs-vee-oo)
DESVIO
detour

What follows are approximate conversions, so when you order something by liters, kilograms or grams you will have an idea of what to expect and not find yourself being handed one piece of candy when you thought you ordered an entire bag.

To Convert			Do the Math		
liters (l) to gallons,	multiply by 0.26		4 liters x 0.26	=	1.04 gallons
gallons to liters,	multiply by 3.79		10 gal. x 3.79	=	37.9 liters
kilograms (kg) to pounds,	multiply by 2.2		2 kilograms x 2.2	=	4.4 pounds
pounds to kilos,	multiply by 0.46		10 pounds x 0.46	=	4.6 kg
grams (g) to ounces,	multiply by 0.035		100 grams x 0.035	=	3.5 oz.
ounces to grams,	multiply by 28.35		10 oz. x 28.35	=	283.5 g.
meters (m) to feet,	multiply by 3.28		2 meters x 3.28	=	6.56 feet
feet to meters,	multiply by 0.3		6 feet x 0.3	=	1.8 meters

For fun, take your weight in pounds and convert it into kilograms. It sounds better that way, doesn't it? How many kilometers is it from your home to school, to work, to the post office?

The Simple Versions		
one liter	=	approximately one US quart
four liters	=	approximately one US gallon
one kilo	=	approximately 2.2 pounds
100 grams	=	approximately 3.5 ounces
500 grams	=	slightly more than one pound
one meter	=	slightly more than three feet

The distance between **Nova York e Rio de Janeiro é** approximately 4,799 miles. How many kilometers would that be? It is 5,745 miles between **Rio de Janeiro e Londres**. How many kilometers is that?

kilometers (km.) to miles,	multiply by 0.62		1000 km. x 0.62	=	620 miles
miles to kilometers,	multiply by 1.6		1000 miles x 1.6	=	1,600 km.

Inches	1		2		3		4		5		6		7

To convert centimeters into inches, multiply by 0.39   Example: 9 cm. x 0.39 = 3.51 in.

To convert inches into centimeters, multiply by 2.54   Example: 4 in. x 2.54 = 10.16 cm.

cm 1	2	3	4	5	6	7	8	9	10	11	12	13	14	15	16	17	18

(seem) (tahm-bame) (ah)
Sim, também há bills to pay **no Brasil e em Portugal. Você** have just finished your delicious
there are

(kair)
dinner **e você quer pagar a conta. O que você faz? Voce chama o garçom ou a garçonete.**
want   do   call   waiter   waitress

(gar-sohm)   (shah-mah) (gar-sohm)   (gar-soh-neh-chee)

(gar-sohm)   *(eh-lee)*
O garçom will normally reel off what **você** have eaten while writing rapidly. **Ele** will then place
waiter

(jee-zair) (sown)   (heh-eyes)   (toh-tahl)
a piece **de papel** on **a mesa e dizer,** "**São trinta reais no total.**" **Você** will pay **o garçom ou**

(ky-shah)
perhaps **você** will pay **o caixa.**
cashier

(noys)
Being a seasoned traveler, **você** know that tipping as **nós** know it **nos Estados Unidos** can vary

from country to country. **No Brasil** a 10% service charge is usually included on **a conta,** but you

can always add a little more for your **garçom sobre a mesa** if you wish. When **você** dine out on

(vee-ah-zhame)
sua viagem, it is always a good idea to make a reservation. It can be difficult to get into a
your   trip

(hehs-tow-rahn-chee)
popular **restaurante.** Nevertheless, the experience is well worth the trouble **você** might

encounter to obtain a reservation. **E** remember, **você sabe** enough **português** to make a
(sah-bee)
know

reservation. Just speak slowly and clearly.

❏ **setembro** *(seh-tem-broo)*	September		
❏ **severo** *(seh-veh-roo)*	severe		
❏ **o silêncio** *(see-lane-see-oo)*	silence	**S**	
❏ **simples** *(seem-pleesh)*	simple		
❏ **simultâneo** *(see-mool-tah-neh-oo)*	simultaneous		

Remember these key **palavras** when dining out, be it **no Brasil ou em Portugal.**

(gar-sohm)
o garçom _____
waiter

(gar-soh-neh-chee)
a garçonete _____
waitress

(kohn-tah)
a conta _____ *a conta, a conta* _____
bill

(gor-zheh-tah)
a gorjeta _____
tip

(kar-dah-pee-oo)   (meh-noo)
o cardápio / o menu _____
menu

(troh-koo)
o troco _____
change

(dehs-kool-pee)
desculpe _____
excuse me

(oh-bree-gah-doo) (oh-bree-gah-dah)
obrigado / obrigada _____
thank you (♂)   thank you (♀)

(fah-vor)
por favor _____
please

(mee) (dah)   (dah-mee)
me dá / da-me _____
give me (Brazil)   give me (Portugal)

(kohn-vair-sah-sown)
Aqui está a sample **conversação** involving paying **a conta** in a hotel.

Carlos: **Por favor, quero pagar a conta.**
                              to pay
_____ *Por favor, quero pagar a conta.* _____

(zheh-rehn-chee)
Gerente: **O número do apartamento, por favor?**
manager   *(noo-meh-roo)   (ah-par-tah-mehn-too)*
                                 hotel room
_____

Carlos: **Apartamento trezentos e dez.**
                    (treh-zehn-toosh)
_____

Gerente: **Obrigado. Um momento senhor.**

_____

Gerente: **Aqui está a conta.**

_____

If **você** have any problems **com números,** just ask someone to write out **os números,** so that

você can be sure you understand everything correctly, **"Por favor, escreva os números!"**
                                                                (es-kreh-vah)
                                                                write out

Practice: _____
(Please write out the numbers! Thank you.)

❏ **a sinfonia** *(seen-foh-nee-ah)* .... symphony _____
❏ **o sistema** *(sees-teh-mah)* .... system _____
❏ **social** *(soh-see-ahl)* .... social _____
❏ **o sofá** *(soh-fah)* .... sofa   **S** _____
❏ **sólido** *(soh-lee-doo)* .... solid _____

70

Agora, let's take a break from **as contas e o dinheiro e** learn some **novas** fun **palavras. Você**

(jeen-yay-roo)
money

can always practice these **palavras** by using your flash cards at the back of this **livro.** Carry

these flash cards in your purse, pocket, briefcase **ou** knapsack **e** *use them!*

(ah-bair-too)
aberto
open

_____

(feh-shah-doo)
fechado
closed

_____

(grahn-jee)
grande
big

_____

(peh-kay-noo)
pequeno
small

_____

(sow-dah-vel)
saudável
healthy

_____

(doh-ehn-chee)
doente
sick

_____

(bohm)
bom
good

_____

(mow)
mau
bad

_____

(kane-chee)
quente
hot

_____

(free-oo)
frio
cold

_____

☐	**o tabaco** *(tah-bah-koo)*	tobacco		_____
☐	**a tarifa** *(tah-ree-fah)*	tariff, fare		_____
☐	**o táxi** *(tahk-see)*	taxi	**t**	_____
☐	**o teatro** *(teh-ah-troo)*	theater		_____
☐	**técnico** *(tek-nee-koo)*	technical		_____

(koor-too)
curto _____

short

(deh-vah-gar)
devagar _____

slow

(ahl-too)
alto _____

tall, high

(vel-yoo)
velho _____

old

(kah-roo)
caro _____

expensive

(hee-koo)
rico _____

rich

(mwee-too)
muito _____

a lot

(lohn-goo)
longo _____

long

(hah-pee-doo)
rápido _____

fast

(by-shoo)
baixo _____

short, low

(zhoh-vame)
jovem _____

young

(bah-rah-too)
barato _____

inexpensive

(poh-bree)
pobre _____

poor

(poh-koo)
pouco _____

a little

❏	**o telefone** *(teh-leh-foh-nee)*	telephone	
❏	**o telegrama** *(teh-leh-grah-mah)*	telegram	
❏	**a televisão** *(teh-leh-vee-zown)*	television	**t**
❏	**a temperatura** *(tame-peh-rah-too-rah)*	temperature	
❏	**o terminal** *(tair-mee-nahl)*	terminal	

(mysh)

Aqui estão mais verbos novos.

(sah-bair)
saber _____
to know (fact) / (how to)

(poh-dair)
poder _____
to be able to, can

(lair)
ler _____
to read

(tair) (kay)
ter que _____
to have to, must

Study the patterns **abaixo** closely, as **você** will use these verbs a lot.

Avenida Atlântica

(sah-bair)
saber
to know (fact), to know (how to)

Eu _sei/_ _____ **tudo.** *(too-doo)*
everything

Você _____ o **endereço.** *(ehn-deh-reh-soo)*
address

Ele _sabe/_ _____ **falar português.** to speak
Ela

Nós _____ o **nome do hotel.**

Eles _____ **falar francês.**
Elas

Meu nome é Elena.

(poh-dair)
poder
to be able to, can

Eu _posso/_ _____ **falar espanhol.** *(es-pahn-yohl)*

Você _pode/_ _____ **entender português.** *(ehn-tehn-dair)* understand

Ele _____ **ler português.** *(lair)* read
Ela

Nós _podemos/_ _____ **falar inglês.**

Eles _podem/_ _____ **entender alemão.** *(ah-leh-mown)*
Elas

(lair)
ler
to read

Eu _leio/_ _____ o **livro.**

Você _lê/_ _____ a **revista.** *(heh-vees-tah)* magazine

Ele _____ o **cardápio.** *(kar-dah-pee-oo)* menu
Ela

Nós _lemos/_ _____ **muito.**

Eles _lêem/_ _____ o **jornal.** *(zhor-nahl)* newspaper
Elas

(tair) (kay)
ter que
to have to, must

Eu _tenho que/_ _____ **aprender português.** *(ah-prehn-dair)*

Você _____ **ler o livro.**

Ele _tem que/_ _____ **comer agora.**
Ela

Nós _____ **visitar a Bahia.**

Eles _têm que/_ _____ **pagar a conta.**
Elas

❏ **o termômetro** *(tair-moh-meh-troo)*	thermometer	_____
❏ **típico** *(chee-pee-koo)*	typical	_____
❏ **o tomate** *toh-mah-chee)*	tomato	**t** _____
❏ **o total** *(toh-tahl)*	total	_____
❏ **o tráfego** *(trah-feh-goo)*	traffic	_____

73

Notice that **"poder," "ter que," e "querer"** can be combined with another verb.

(kair-oo)
Eu quero pagar.
want
(koh-mair)
Eu quero comer.
to eat

(noys) (poh-deh-moosh) (lair)
Nós podemos ler português.
can

Nós podemos pagar a conta.

(tame) (eer)
Ele tem que ir.
must / has to   go

Ele tem que pagar a conta.

(kair-oo) (ah-prehn-dair) (por-too-gaysh)
Quero aprender português.
(I) want

Posso aprender português.
(I) can

Tenho que aprender português.
(I) must

(poh-jee)
Você pode translate the sentences **para o português ? As respostas estão abaixo.**
can   into
(ah-by-shoo)

1. I can speak Portuguese. _____

2. They can pay the bill. _____

3. He has to pay the bill. _____

4. We know the answer. _____ *Nós sabemos a resposta.* _____

5. She knows a lot. _____

6. We can read Portuguese. _____

7. I cannot eat a lot. _____

8. We are not able to (cannot) understand French. _____

9. I want to visit Lisbon. _____

10. She reads the newspaper. _____

Agora, draw **linhas** *(leen-yahs)* **entre** *(ehn-tree)* the opposites **abaixo.** *(ah-by-shoo)* **Não** forget to say them out loud. Use these **palavras** every day to describe **coisas** *(koy-zahs)* **em sua casa, em sua escola** *(es-koh-lah)* **e em seu** *(seh-oo)* **escritório.**

your *school* *your* *office*

(grahn-jee) **grande**

(es-kair-dah) **esquerda**

(zhoh-vame) **jovem**

(poh-bree) **pobre**

(sow-dah-vel) **saudável**

(lohn-goo) **longo**

(mwee-too) **muito**

(bohm) **bom**

(kane-chee) **quente**

(ehm-by-shoo) **embaixo**

(deh-vah-gar) **devagar**

(kah-roo) **caro**

(feh-shah-doo) **fechado**

(ehm) *(see-mah)* **em cima**

(ah-bair-too) **aberto**

(koor-too) **curto**

(bah-rah-too) **barato**

(poh-koo) **pouco**

(doh-ehn-chee) **doente**

(hah-pee-doo) **rápido**

(vel-yoo) **velho**

(peh-kay-noo) **pequeno**

(jee-ray-tah) **direita**

(free-oo) **frio**

(hee-koo) **rico**

(mow) **mau**

Futebol *(foo-cheh-bohl)* **é** the most popular sport **no Brasil. Nos domingos você** will see thousands of fans

soccer

streaming to their local club **ou para a Maracanã no Rio.** Even if **futebol** *(foo-cheh-bohl)* is not your favorite

esporte, *(es-por-chee)* don't miss **a oportunidade** *(oh-por-too-nee-dah-jee)* to join in.

sport *opportunity*

❏ **trágico** *(trah-zhee-koo)*	. . . .	tragic	_____
❏ **tranqüilo** *(trahn-kwee-loo)*	. . . .	tranquil, quiet	_____
❏ **transparente** *(trahns-pah-rehn-chee)*	. . . .	transparent	**t** _____
❏ **transportar** *(trahns-por-tar)*	. . . .	to transport	_____
❏ **o trem** *(trame)*	. . . .	train	_____

75

(vee-ah-zhar)
Viajar, Viajar, Viajar
to travel

(ohn-tame)   *(brah-zee-lee-ah)*
Ontem em Brasília!
yesterday

(oh-zhee)   *(hee-oo)*
Hoje no Rio!
today

(ah-mahn-yahn)   *(sown)* *(pow-loo)*
Amanhã em São Paulo!
tomorrow

If you know a few key **palavras,** traveling can be easy in both **Brasil e Portugal. O português** is

spoken by millions of people around the world with each country adding its own character **e** flavor

to the language. Keep in mind that **Brasil** alone has a population of over 190 million people!

(vee-ah-zhah)
Como você viaja?

Pedro viaja *(vee-ah-zhah) (jee) (kar-hoo)* **de carro.**
travels

Cláudia viaja *(klow-jee-ah) (jee) (trame)* **de trem.**

Ana viaja de avião. *(ah-vee-own)*
airplane

José viaja de barco. *(zhoh-zeh) (bar-koo)*
boat

João viaja de motocicleta. *(zhoh-own) (moh-toh-see-kleh-tah)*

Maria viaja de ônibus. *(ow-nee-boos)*

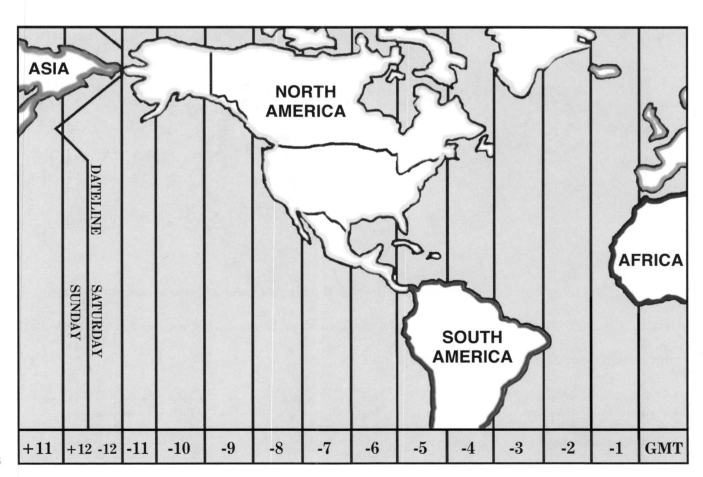

ASIA	DATELINE			NORTH AMERICA						SOUTH AMERICA				AFRICA
+11	+12	-12	-11	-10	-9	-8	-7	-6	-5	-4	-3	-2	-1	GMT

Quando você are traveling, **você** will want to tell others your nationality **e você** will meet people from all corners of the world. Can you guess where someone is from if they say one of the following? **As respostas** are in your glossary beginning on page 108.

Eu sou da Inglaterra. _____
am from

Sou da Itália. _____

(peh-roo)
Sou do Peru. _____

Sou da Espanha. _____

(bel-zhee-kah)
Sou da Bélgica. _____

(swee-sah)
Sou da Suíça. _____

(ohn-doo-rahs)
Sou de Honduras. _____

Sou da Bolívia. _____

(ar-zhehn-chee-nah)
Sou da Argentina. _____

(noys)   *(frahn-sah)*
Nós somos da França. _____

(ah-leh-mahn-yah)
Somos da Alemanha. _____

(meh-shee-koo)
Somos do México. _____

(hee-kah)
Somos da Costa Rica. _____

(shee-lee)
Ela é do Chile. _____

(koo-bah)
Ele é de Cuba. _____

Ela é de Portugal. _____

(ows-trah-lee-ah)
Ele é da Austrália. _____

Eu sou do Canadá. _____

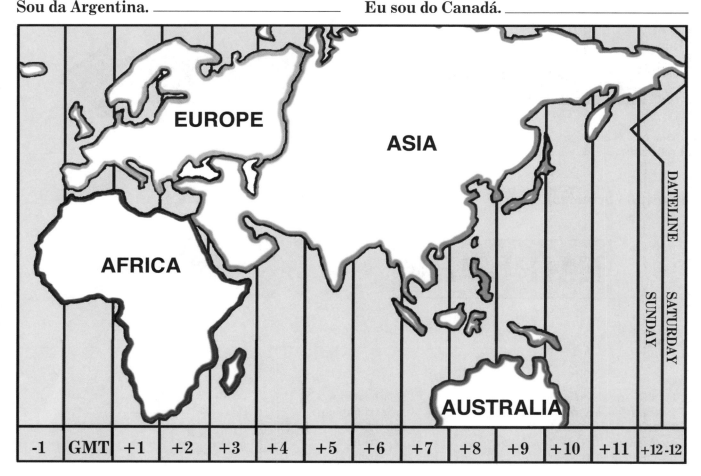

| -1 | GMT | +1 | +2 | +3 | +4 | +5 | +6 | +7 | +8 | +9 | +10 | +11 | +12 -12 |

A palavra for "trip" is taken from **a palavra** *(vee-ah-zhar)* **"viajar,"** which makes it easy: **a viagem.** *(vee-ah-zhame)* **Muitas**
to travel the trip
(kair)
palavras revolve around the concept of travel, which is exactly what **você quer** to do. Practice

the following **palavras** many times. **Você** will see them often.

(vee-ah-zhar)
viajar _____
to travel

(ah-zhayn-see-ah) (jeh) (vee-ah-zhehns)
a agência de viagens _____
travel agency

(vee-ah-zhahn-chee)
o viajante _____
traveler

(boh-ah) (vee-ah-zhame)
Boa viagem! _____
have a good trip

(kar-hoo)
If **você** choose **viajar de carro, aqui estão** a few key **palavras.**

(es-trah-dah)
a estrada _____
road

(kar-hoo) (ah-loo-gah-doo)
o carro alugado _____
rental car

(ow-too-es-trah-dah)
a auto-estrada _____
freeway

(ah-loo-gehl) (kar-hoosh)
o aluguél de carros _____
car-rental agency

(hoo-ah)
a rua _____
street

(pohs-too) (gah-zoh-lee-nah)
o posto de gasolina _____
service station

(ah)
Abaixo há some basic signs which **você** should **também** learn to recognize quickly.
there are

(ehn-trar)
entrar _____
to enter

(sah-eer)
sair _____
to exit

ENTRADA ▶

SAÍDA ▶

(ehn-trah-dah)
a entrada _____
entrance

(sah-ee-dah)
a saída _____
exit

(preen-see-pahl)
a entrada principal _____
main

(eh-mair-zhayn-see-ah)
a saída de emergência _____
emergency

EMPURRE

PUXE

(ehm-poor-hee)
empurre _____
push (doors)

(poo-shee)
puxe _____
pull (doors)

❑	**o triângulo** *(tree-ahn-goo-loo)*	triangle	_____
❑	**triunfante** *(tree-oon-fahn-chee)*	triumphant	_____
❑	**trivial** *(tree-vee-ahl)*	trivial	**t** _____
❑	**a trompeta** *(trohm-peh-tah)*	trumpet	_____
❑	**tropical** *(troh-pee-kahl)*	tropical	_____

Let's learn the basic travel verbs. Take out a piece of paper **e** make up your own sentences with these **palavras novas.** Follow the same pattern **você** have in previous Steps. The patterns for the verb **"ir"** and **"fazer"** are on page 66.

(ah)
há*
there is, there are

(sheh-gar)
chegar
to arrive

(par-cheer)
partir
to depart

(peh-jeer)
pedir
to order, to request

(eer) (jee) (kar-hoo)
ir de carro
to drive, to go by car

(eer) (jee) (ah-vee-own)
ir de avião
to fly, to go by plane

(fah-zair)   (mah-lah)
fazer a mala
to pack   suitcase

(troh-kar)
trocar
to transfer (vehicles), to change (money)

* This verb doesn't need to be conjugated. It stays the same.

(ah)
Aqui há some **palavras novas para a** **viagem.**
(vee-ah-zhame)
trip

(ah-air-oh-por-too)
o aeroporto
airport

(plah-tah-for-mah)
a plataforma
platform

(oh-rah-ree-oo)
o horário
timetable

DO RIO À SÃO PAULO		
Partida	Nº do trem	Chegada
00:41	50	09:41
07:40	19	16:40
12:15	22	21:15
14:32	10	23:32
21:40	04	06:40

(es-tah-sown) (jee) (trame)
a estação de trem
train station

❏ **o tumulto** *(too-mool-too)* .... tumult
❏ **o túnel** *(too-nel)* .... tunnel
❏ **o/a turista** *(too-rees-tah)* .... tourist
❏ **o turismo** *(too-rees-moo)* .... tourism
❏ **o tutor** *(too-tor)* .... tutor

t

Com estas palavras, você está *(es-tahs)* ready for any **viagem**, anywhere. **Você** should have no problem
com these verbs **novos**, just remember the basic "plug-in" formula **você** have already learned.
Use that knowledge to translate the following thoughts **para o português.** *(into)* **As respostas estão**
abaixo.

1. I fly to Rio. _____

2. I transfer (planes) in São Paulo. _____

3. He drives to Fortaleza. _____ *Ele vai de carro para Fortaleza.* _____

4. We leave tomorrow. _____

5. We buy tickets to Manaus. _____

6. They drive to Minas Gerais. _____

7. Where is the plane to Vitória? _____

8. How can I go to Portugal? With Air TAP or with Varig? _____

Aqui há some **palavras** *(eem-por-tahn-chees)* **importantes** *(vee-ah-zhahn-chee)* **para o viajante.**
traveler

RIO - MANAUS		
Partida	Nº do trem	Chegada
00:41	50	09:41
07:40	19	16:40
12:15	22	21:15
14:32	10	23:32
21:40	04	06:40

(oh-koo-pah-doo)
ocupado _____
occupied

(lee-vree)
livre _____
free

(vah-gown)
o vagão _____
compartment, wagon

(ahs-sehn-too)
o assento _____
seat

(par-chee-dah)
a partida _____
departure

(sheh-gah-dah)
a chegada _____
arrival

(een-tair-nah-see-oh-nahl)
internacional _____
foreign, international

(doh-mehs-chee-koo)
doméstico _____
domestic, internal (of the country)

Increase your travel **palavras** by writing out **as palavras abaixo e** practicing the sample sentences out loud. Practice asking *(pair-goon-tahs)* **perguntas com "onde."** It will help you later.

(pah-rah)
para _____
to   Onde está o avião para Iguaçu?

(ah-vee-own)
o avião _____
plane   Onde está o avião para Brasília?

(por-town)
o portão _____
gate   Onde é o portão número oito?

(bahl-kown)
o balcão _____
counter   Onde é o balcão número nove?

(seh-sown)   *(pair-jee-doosh)*   *(ah-shah-doosh)*
a seção de perdidos e achados _____
lost-and-found office   Onde é a seção de perdidos e achados?

(kar-heh-gah-dor)
o carregador *Onde está o carregador?*
porter   Onde está o carregador?

(heh-seh-bee-mehn-too) (jee) (bah-gah-zhame)
o recebimento de bagagem _____
baggage claim   Onde é o recebimento de bagagem?

(ah-zhayn-see-ah) (jeh) (kahm-bee-oo)
a agência de câmbio _____
money-exchange office   Onde há uma agência de câmbio?

(sah-lah)   *(es-peh-rah)*
a sala de espera _____
waiting room   Onde é a sala de espera?

(kor-heh-dor)
o corredor _____
aisle   Eu quero um assento no corredor.

(zhah-neh-lah)
a janela _____
window   Eu quero um assento na janela.

(seh-sown) (jee) (nown) (foo-mahn-chees)
a seção de não fumantes _____
non-smoking section   Há uma seção de não fumantes?

_____ *(sheh-gah)* **chega o trem?**   _____ *(vy)* **vai?**
(when)   (when)   (how)   (how)

❐ **último** *(ool-chee-moo)*	. . . .	ultimate, last	_____
❐ **a união** *(oo-nee-own)*	. . . .	union	_____
❐ **o uniforme** *(oo-nee-for-mee)*	. . . .	uniform	**u** _____
❐ **a universidade** *(oo-nee-vair-see-dah-jee)*	. . . . .	university	_____
❐ **urgente** *(oor-zhehn-chee)*	. . . .	urgent	_____

Você pode ler as seguintes frases?
(poh-jee) can   read   *(seh-geen-chees)* following   *(frah-zeesh)* phrases

Agora você está **sentado** no **avião** e você **vai**
(sehn-tah-doo) seated   *(ah-vee-own)*   go/fly

de avião para o Brasil. Você tem o dinheiro, as

passagens, o **passaporte** e as **malas**. Você tem
(pahs-sah-por-chee)   suitcases

um assento no corredor. Ele tem um assento na

janela. Agora você é turista. Você **chega**
(sheh-gah)

amanhã às 8:00. Boa viagem! Boa sorte!

Não há muitos trens no Brasil. Because of its size, **você** will probably use **aviões** to get from
(ah-vee-oynsh) planes

one end of the country to the other. However, **há trens entre** some cities. **No Rio há também** a
(ah) there is

cogwheel **trem** that goes up to **Corcovado.** It is most likely that **você** will do most of your
(kor-koh-vah-doo)

traveling either **de ônibus ou de avião.**

❑ **usado** *(oo-zah-doo)*	used	
❑ **usar** *(oo-zar)*	to use	
❑ **usual** *(oo-zoo-ahl)*	usual	**u**
❑ **o utensílio** *(oo-tehn-see-lee-oo)*	utensil	
❑ **a utilidade** *(oo-chee-lee-dah-jee)*	utility	

Knowing these travel **palavras** will make your holiday twice as enjoyable **e** at least three times as easy. Drill yourself on this Step by selecting other destinations **e** ask your own **perguntas** about **trens, ônibus, ou aviões** *(ah-vee-oynsh)* that go there. Select **as palavras novas de** your **dicionário** *(jee-see-oh-nah-ree-oo)* **e** ask your own questions beginning with **<u>quando</u>, <u>onde</u>, e <u>quanto custa</u>.** **As respostas** to the crossword puzzle are at the bottom of the next page.

ACROSS

1. (I) read
6. ladies (restroom)
7. platform
9. well
10. to know
11. tip
14. (I) need
17. to enter
18. time
19. what
23. monetary unit of **Brasil**
25. restaurant
27. to travel
28. to buy
31. to write
33. cold
34. she
35. nothing
36. (I) want

DOWN

1. pencil
2. one hundred
3. station
4. to do, to make
5. bad
6. sick
8. to repeat
12. hotel room
13. excuse me
15. computer
16. to drink
20. suitcase
21. to leave, to depart
22. bill
24. to say
26. number
29. give me
30. open
32. twenty
33. to speak

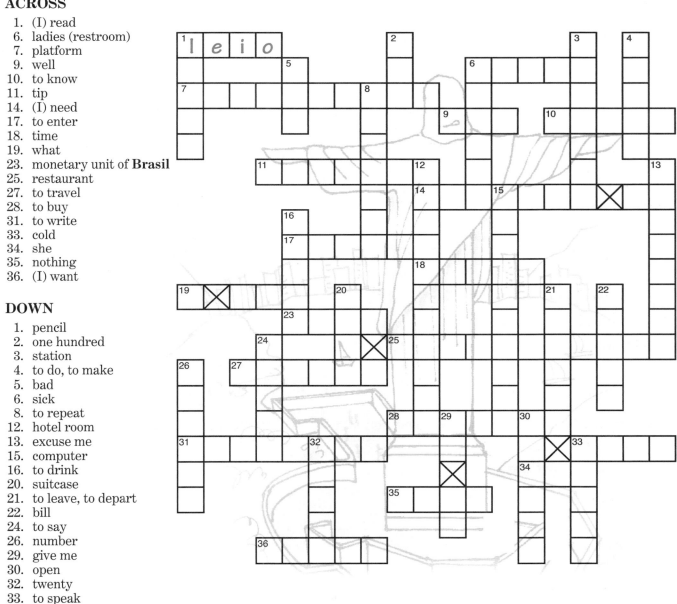

Corcovado is **uma montanha no Rio.** At its summit is the familiar statue of **Cristo Redentor.** It is this image which has become symbolic of the **cidade** of **Rio de Janeiro.**

❏ **a vacina** *(vah-see-nah)*	vaccine	_____
❏ **a vaga** *(vah-gah)*	vacancy	_____
❏ **válido** *(vah-lee-doo)*	valid	**V** _____
❏ **o vegetariano** *(veh-zheh-tah-ree-ah-noo)*	vegetarian	_____
❏ **a vista** *(vees-tah)*	view	_____

What about inquiring about the price of **passagens?** *(pahs-sah-zhehns)* **Você pode** *(poh-jee)* ask these **perguntas.**
tickets   can

Quanto custa uma passagem para a Bahia? *(bah-ee-ah)* _____

Quanto custa uma passagem para o Paraná? _____

Quanto custa uma passagem para a Lisboa? *(lees-boh-ah)* _____

a passagem de ida *(pahs-sah-zhame) (jee) (ee-dah)* _____
one-way ticket

a passagem de ida e volta *(vohl-tah)* _____
round-trip ticket

What about times of **partida e chegada?** *(par-chee-dah) (sheh-gah-dah)* **Você pode perguntar isso também!**
departure arrival   ask

A que horas parte o avião para Manaus? *(par-chee) (ah-vee-own) (mah-nows)* _____
at what time departs

A que horas parte o avião para Londres? *(lohn-dreesh)* _____

A que horas chega o avião de Santiago? *(sheh-gah)* _____
arrives

A que horas chega o avião de Angola? _____

A que horas parte o avião para São Paulo? *(par-chee)* _____

Você have just arrived **no Brasil. Você está no aeroporto.** *(ah-air-oh-por-too)* **Onde você quer ir?** *(kair) (eer)* **Para São**

Paulo? Para Minas? Tell that to the person at **o balção** *(bahl-kown)* selling **passagens!**
counter

Quero ir para Fortaleza. *(kair-oo) (eer)* _____
go

A que horas parte o avião para Fortaleza? _____

Quanto custa uma passagem para Fortaleza? _____

Agora that **você** know the words essential for traveling – be it throughout **Brasil ou Portugal,** what are some speciality items **você** might go in search of?

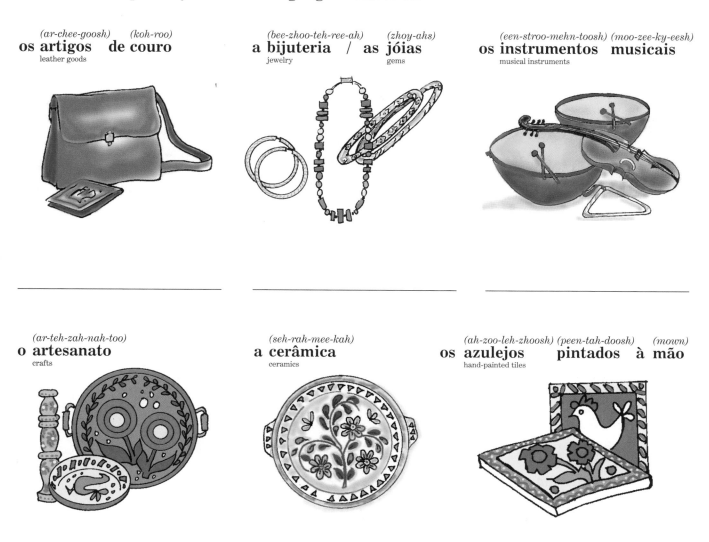

(ar-chee-goosh) *(koh-roo)*
os artigos de couro
leather goods

(bee-zhoo-teh-ree-ah) *(zhoy-ahs)*
a bijuteria / as jóias
jewelry gems

(een-stroo-mehn-toosh) (moo-zee-ky-eesh)
os instrumentos musicais
musical instruments

(ar-teh-zah-nah-too)
o artesanato
crafts

(seh-rah-mee-kah)
a cerâmica
ceramics

(ah-zoo-leh-zhoosh) (peen-tah-doosh) (mown)
os azulejos pintados à mão
hand-painted tiles

Consider using PORTUGUESE *a language map*® as well. PORTUGUESE *a language map*® is the perfect companion for your travels when **você** may not wish to take along this **livro.** Each

(vee-ah-zhame)
section focuses on essentials for your **viagem.** Your *Language Map*® is not meant to replace learning **português**, but will help you in the event **você** forget something and need a little bit of help. For more information about the *Language Map*® Series, please go to www.bbks.com.

❑ **o vale** *(vah-lee)*	valley		
❑ **a vaidade** *(vy-dah-jee)*	vanity		
❑ **vários** *(vah-ree-oosh)*	various	**V**	
❑ **o vaso** *(vah-zoo)*	vase		
❑ **o Vaticano** *(vah-chee-kah-noo)*	the Vatican		

(ah-par-tah-mehn-too)   *(foh-mee)*

Você está agora no Brasil ou em Portugal e você tem um **apartamento.** Você está com **fome.**
        hotel room   hunger

(ah)   *(ah)*

Onde há um bom **restaurante?** First of all, **há** different types of places to eat. Let's learn them.
 is there   there are

(hehs-tow-rahn-chee)

o restaurante _____

            exactly what it says with a variety of meals

(kah-fay)

o café _____

            a coffee house **com** snacks **e** beverages

(lahn-shoh-neh-chee)

a lanchonete _____

            a type of **restaurante** where you find assorted

            sandwiches, snacks, ice cream **e** beverages.

(bar-zeen-yoo)

o barzinho _____

      a local street bar that generally stays open all day. People step in to have a **cafezinho**

      ou chope as well as other beverages. Snacks **e** phone cards can also be purchased here.
        draft beer

(kah-fay-zeen-yoo)

"Cafezinho" is that little espresso-type drink which Brazilians drink over the counter **no**

(ah-soo-kar)

barzinho ou after any meal. **É** generally served black **com** some **açúcar.**
                                          sugar

(bohm)   *(ah-peh-chee-chee)*

Before beginning your meal, be sure to wish those sharing your table – "**Bom apetite!**" Your
                                                  enjoy your meal

turn to practice now.

_____

            (enjoy your meal)

And at least one more time for practice!

_____

            (enjoy your meal)

❑ **o veículo** *(veh-ee-koo-loo)*	vehicle	_____
❑ **o vinagre** *(vee-nah-gree)*	vinegar	_____
❑ **o vinho** *(veen-yoo)*	wine	**v** _____
❑ **o violino** *(vee-oh-lee-noo)*	violin	_____
❑ **a visa** *(vee-zah)*	visa	_____

Start imagining now all the new taste treats you will experience abroad. Try all of the different types of eating establishments mentioned on the previous page. Experiment. If **você**

(ehn-kohn-trar)
encontrar um restaurante that **você** would like to try, consider calling ahead to make **uma**

(heh-zair-vah)
reserva:
reservation

(kair-oo) *(heh-zair-var)* *(meh-zah)*
"**Quero reservar uma mesa, por favor.**"
to reserve

_____

(I want to reserve a table, please.)

If **você precisa de um cardápio**, catch the attention of **o garçom**, saying,

> "**Garçom. O cardápio, por favor!**"

_____

(Waiter. The menu please!)

If your **garçom** asks if **você** enjoyed your meal, a smile **e** a "**Sim, muito obrigado,**" will tell him that you did.

(hehs-tow-rahn-chees) *(brah-zee-lay-roosh)*
Most **restaurantes brasileiros** post **o cardápio** outside **ou** inside. Do not hesitate to ask to see

(heh-fay-soynsh) *(preh-soos)*
o cardápio before being seated so **você sabe** what type of **refeições e preços você** will encounter.
meals prices

(es-peh-see-ahl) *(jee-ah)* *(prah-too)*
Most **restaurantes** offer **um** "**especial do dia.**" Some **restaurantes** also offer **um** "**prato**
special meal of the day

(fay-too) *(heh-fay-sown)*
feito" at lunchtime. This is a complete **refeição,** chosen by the chef for that day, usually at a
meal

(preh-soo)
very reasonable **preço.**
price

❐	**a visita** *(vee-zee-tah)*	visit	**v**	_____
❐	**visitar** *(vee-zee-tar)*	to visit		_____
❐	**o zodíaco** *(zoh-jee-ah-koo)*	zodiac		_____
❐	**a zona** *(zoh-nah)*	zone	**z**	_____
❐	**a zoologia** *(zoh-oh-loh-zhee-ah)*	zoology		_____

No Brasil e em Portugal há *there are* **três** main meals to enjoy every day, plus perhaps **doces** *(doh-seesh)* *pastry* **para** *for* the

tired traveler in **à tarde**. *afternoon*

o café da manhã *(kah-fay) (mahn-yahn)* / **o pequeno almoço** *(peh-kay-noo) (ahl-moh-soo)* _____
breakfast (Brazil)   *breakfast (Portugal)*

Em hotéis *(oh-tay-ees)* **e pousadas** *(poh-zah-dahs)* this meal usually consists of coffee, tea, fresh orange juice, **pão,** butter,
hotels   *inns*

cheese **e** fruit. Check serving times before **você** retire for the night or you might miss out!

o almoço *(ahl-moh-soo)* _____
lunch
               generally served from 12:00 to 15:00

o jantar *(zhahn-tar)* _____
dinner
               generally served from 20:00 to midnight

Agora for a preview of delights to come . . . At the back of this **livro, você** will find a sample

cardápio *(kar-dah-pee-oo)* **brasileiro** *(brah-zee-lay-roo)*. **Leia** *(lay-ah)* **o cardápio hoje** *(oh-zhee)* **e aprenda** *(ah-prehn-dah)* **as palavras novas!** When **você** are
read   *today*   *learn*

ready to leave on your **viagem,** *(vee-ah-zhame)* cut out **o cardápio**, fold it, **e** carry it in your pocket, wallet **ou**

purse. Before you go, how do **você** say these **três** phrases which are **muito importantes para**

the hungry **viajante?** *(vee-ah-zhahn-chee)*
traveler

Excuse me. I want to reserve a table, please. _____

Waiter! A menu, please! _____

Enjoy your meal! _____

_____ **come a salada?**   _____ **bebe o suco?** *(soo-koo)*
(who)   *eats*   *(who)*   *juice*

_____ **viaja** *(vee-ah-zhah)* **para Angola?**
(who)

(who)

Learning the following should help you to identify what kind of meat **você** have ordered **e como** it will be prepared.

- ❐ **vaca** *(vah-kah)* . . . . beef   _____
- ❐ **vitela** *(vee-teh-lah)* . . . . veal   _____
- ❐ **porco** *(por-koo)* . . . . pork   _____
- ❐ **carneiro** *(kar-nay-roo)* . . . . mutton   _____

O cardápio below has the main categories **você** will find in most restaurants. Learn them **hoje** *(oh-zhee)* so that **você** will easily recognize them when you dine **em Portugal ou no Brasil.** Be sure to write the words in the blanks below.

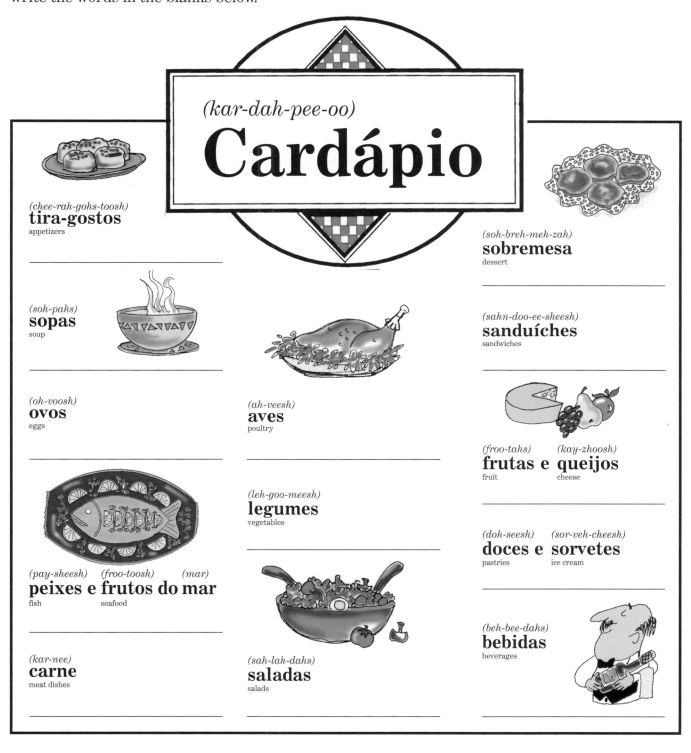

(kar-dah-pee-oo)
Cardápio

(chee-rah-gohs-toosh)
tira-gostos
appetizers

_____

(soh-pahs)
sopas
soup

_____

(oh-voosh)
ovos
eggs

(ah-veesh)
aves
poultry

(pay-sheesh) *(froo-toosh)* *(mar)*
peixes e frutos do mar
fish   seafood

_____

(kar-nee)
carne
meat dishes

_____

(leh-goo-meesh)
legumes
vegetables

(sah-lah-dahs)
saladas
salads

_____

(soh-breh-meh-zah)
sobremesa
dessert

_____

(sahn-doo-ee-sheesh)
sanduíches
sandwiches

_____

(froo-tahs) *(kay-zhoosh)*
frutas e queijos
fruit   cheese

_____

(doh-seesh) *(sor-veh-cheesh)*
doces e sorvetes
pastries   ice cream

_____

(beh-bee-dahs)
bebidas
beverages

❏	**frango** *(frahn-goo)*	chicken	_____
❏	**cordeiro** *(kor-day-roo)*	lamb	_____
❏	**churrasco** *(shoor-hahs-koo)*	barbeque	_____
❏	**frito** *(free-too)*	fried	_____
❏	**assado** *(ahs-sah-doo)*	roasted	_____

Você também will get **legumes** com your **refeição,** e perhaps **uma salada mista. Um dia**
(tahm-bame) *(leh-goo-meesh)* *(heh-fay-sown)* *(mees-tah)*
vegetables   meal   mixed

at an open-air **feira** will teach you **os nomes** for all the different kinds of **legumes e frutas,**
(fay-rah)
market

plus it will be a delightful experience for you. **Você pode** always consult your menu guide at the
(poh-jee)

back of this **livro** if **você** forget **os nomes corretos. Agora você** are seated **e o garçom** arrives.
(kor-heh-toosh)
waiter

O **café da manhã é um pouco diferente** because **é** fairly standardized **e você** will frequently
(mahn-yahn) *(poh-koo)* *(jee-feh-rehn-chee)*
breakfast   little

take it at your **pousada** as **está incluído no preço do quarto. Abaixo** is a sample of what
(poh-zah-dah) *(een-kloo-ee-doo)* *(preh-soo)*
guest house   (it) is   included   price   room

você pode expect to greet you **de manhã.**

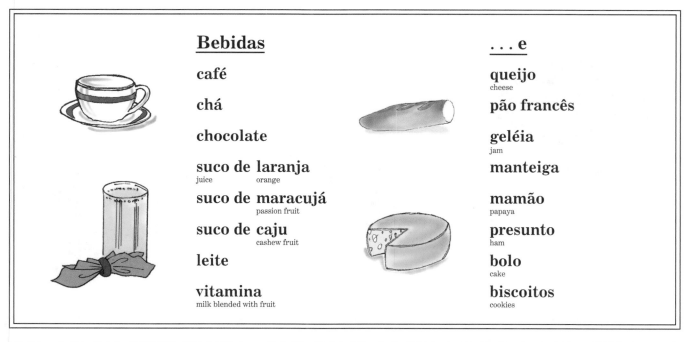

Bebidas   . . . e

café   **queijo**
cheese

chá   **pão francês**

chocolate   **geléia**
jam

suco de laranja   **manteiga**
juice   orange

suco de maracujá   **mamão**
passion fruit   papaya

suco de caju   **presunto**
cashew fruit   ham

leite   **bolo**
cake

vitamina   **biscoitos**
milk blended with fruit   cookies

❑ **cozido** *(koh-zee-doo)*	cooked	_____
❑ **cozido no vapor** *(koh-zee-doo)(noh)(vah-por)*	steamed	_____
❑ **ao forno** *(ah-oh)(for-noo)*	baked	_____
❑ **grelhado** *(grel-yah-doo)*	grilled	_____
❑ **à milanesa** *(ah)(mee-lah-neh-zah)*	in batter	_____

Aqui está an example of what **você** might select for your evening meal. Using your menu guide on pages 117 and 118, as well as what **você** have learned in this Step, fill in the blanks *in English* with what **você** believe your **garçom** will bring you. **As respostas estão** below.

_{answers}

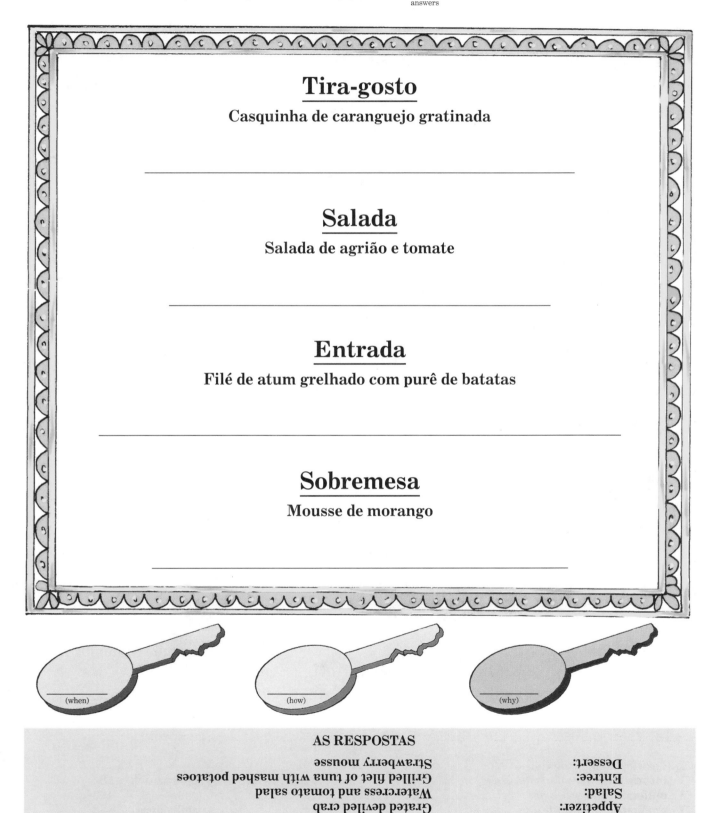

Tira-gosto
Casquinha de caranguejo gratinada

_____

Salada
Salada de agrião e tomate

_____

Entrada
Filé de atum grelhado com purê de batatas

_____

Sobremesa
Mousse de morango

_____

_____ (when)   _____ (how)   _____ (why)

Agora é a good time for a quick review. Draw lines between **as palavras portuguesas e** their English equivalents.

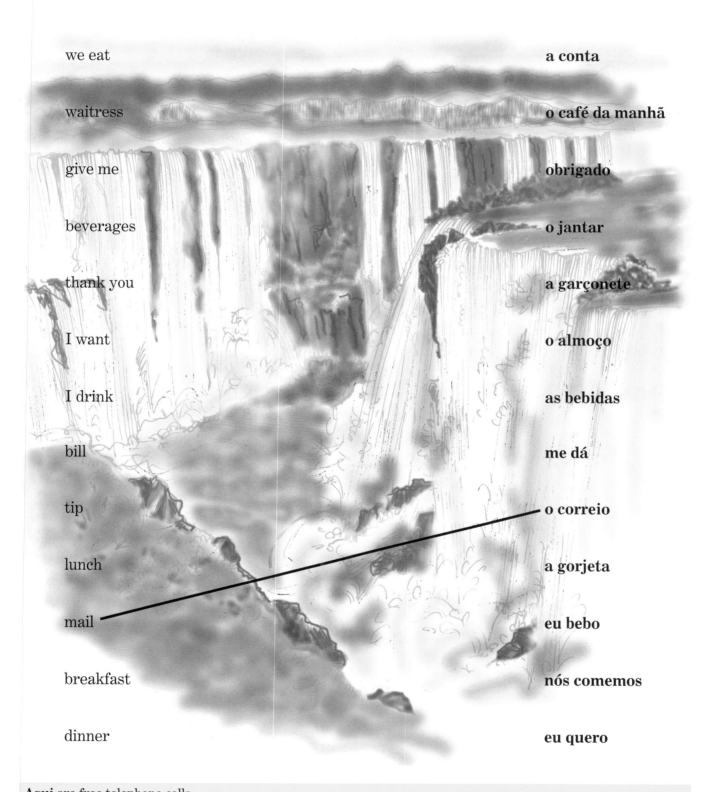

we eat	**a conta**
waitress	**o café da manhã**
give me	**obrigado**
beverages	**o jantar**
thank you	**a garçonete**
I want	**o almoço**
I drink	**as bebidas**
bill	**me dá**
tip	**o correio**
lunch	**a gorjeta**
mail	**eu bebo**
breakfast	**nós comemos**
dinner	**eu quero**

Aqui are free telephone calls.
- ❏ **informação** *(een-for-mah-sown)* . . . . information   102
- ❏ **polícia** *(poh-lee-see-ah)* . . . . police   190
- ❏ **ambulância** *(ahm-boo-lahn-see-ah)* . . . . ambulance   192
- ❏ **incêndio** *(een-same-jee-oo)* . . . . fire   193

What is different about **o telefone no Brasil ou em Portugal?** Well, **você** never notice such

things until **você quer** *(kair)* to use them. **Os telefones** *(teh-leh-foh-neesh)* allow you to call **amigos,** *(ah-mee-goosh)* reserve **ingressos**
friends   tickets

de teatro, de balé, *(bah-lay)* **ou de concerto,** make calls **de urgência,** *(oor-zhayn-see-ah)* check on the hours of **um**
ballet   urgency

museu, *(moo-zeh-oo)* rent **um carro, e** all those other things which **nós fazemos** *(fah-zeh-moosh)* on a daily basis. It **também**
do

gives you a certain amount of freedom when **você pode fazer** your own calls.
make

Are you taking your cell phone with you?

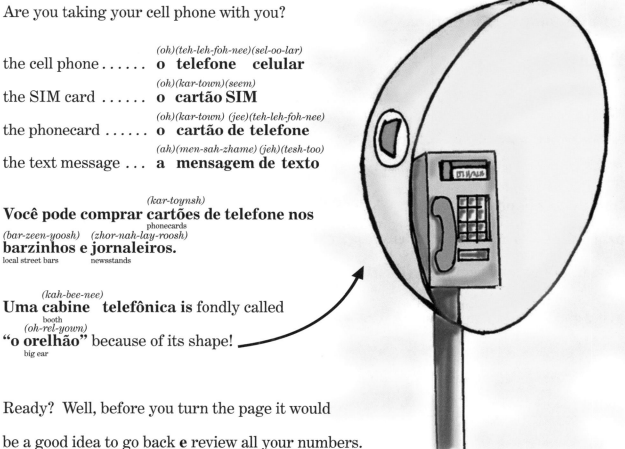

the cell phone	*(oh)(teh-leh-foh-nee)(sel-oo-lar)* **o telefone celular**	
the SIM card	*(oh)(kar-town)(seem)* **o cartão SIM**	
the phonecard	*(oh)(kar-town) (jee)(teh-leh-foh-nee)* **o cartão de telefone**	
the text message . . .	*(ah)(men-sah-zhame) (jeh)(tesh-too)* **a mensagem de texto**	

Você pode comprar cartões de telefone nos *(kar-toynsh)*
phonecards
barzinhos e jornaleiros. *(bar-zeen-yoosh)* *(zhor-nah-lay-roosh)*
local street bars   newsstands

Uma cabine telefônica is fondly called *(kah-bee-nee)*
booth
"o orelhão" because of its shape! *(oh-rel-yown)*
big ear

Ready? Well, before you turn the page it would

be a good idea to go back **e** review all your numbers.

To dial from the United States to most other countries **você** need that country's international

area code. Your **lista telefônica** *(lees-tah)* at home should have a listing of international area codes.
telephone book

Aqui are some **muito** useful words built around the word, **"telefone."**

❐   **a telefonista** *(teh-leh-foh-nees-tah)* . . . . operator   _____

❐   **a cabine telefônica** *(kah-bee-nee)(teh-leh-foh-nee-kah)* . . . . telephone booth   _____

❐   **a lista telefônica** *(lees-tah)(teh-leh-foh-nee-kah)* . . . . telephone book   _____

❐   **a conversação telefônica** *(kohn-vair-sah-sown)(teh-leh-foh-nee-kah)* telephone conversation   _____

When **você** leave your contact numbers with friends, family **ou** business colleagues, **você** should include your destination country's area code **e** city code whenever possible. For example,

Country Codes		City Codes	
Brazil	55	São Paulo	11
		Rio	21
		Brasília	61
		Salvador	71
Portugal	351	Lisboa	21

To call from one city to another city while abroad, **você** may need to call **a telefonista** *(teh-leh-foh-nees-tah)* operator in your hotel. Tell **a telefonista,** "**Eu gostaria** *(gohs-tah-ree-ah)* would like **de telefonar para Recife,**" *(heh-see-fee)* **ou** "**Gostaria de telefonar para Salvador.**"

Now you try it: _____

(I would like to call to Belem.)

When answering **o telefone,** pick up the receiver **e** say, "**Alô?**" *(ah-loh)* The person calling will probably say, "**Alô. Quem fala?**" *(kame)* Be ready to respond with, "**Aqui é** _____ ."

(your name)

Com números de telefone the number **seis (6)** is replaced with "**meia.**" *(may-ah)* **Meia** *(may-ah)* stands for **meia-dúzia.** *(may-ah-doo-zee-ah)* half-dozen So if your **número de telefone** is 246-6205, **você** would say "**dois-quatro-meia-meia-dois-zero-cinco.**" Now **você** say it: **dois** ____ ____ ____ ____ ____ ____

2   4   6   6   2   0   5

When saying good-bye, say "**até logo,**" *(ah-teh) (loh-goo)* until then or "**até amanhã,**" until tomorrow or simply "**tchau.**" *(chow)* good-bye

Your turn —

_____

(Hello. Here is . . .)

_____   _____

(until then)   (until tomorrow)

Do not forget that **você pode perguntar** *(pair-goon-tar)* ask . . .

Quanto custa uma chamada para os Estados Unidos? call _____

Quanto custa uma chamada para a Inglaterra? _____

Here are some countries **você** may wish to call.

- ☐ **a Argentina** *(ar-zhehn-chee-nah)* . . . . Argentina _____
- ☐ **a Bolívia** *(boh-lee-vee-ah)* . . . . Bolivia _____
- ☐ **o Chile** *(shee-lee)* . . . . Chile _____
- ☐ **a Colômbia** *(koh-lohm-bee-ah)* . . . . Colombia _____

Aqui estão some sample telephone phrases. Write them in the blanks **abaixo.**

(gohs-tah-ree-ah)   *(teh-leh-foh-nar)*
Eu gostaria   de telefonar para Miami. _____
would like

(vah-reeg)   *(ah-air-oh-por-too)*
Gostaria de telefonar para a Varig no aeroporto. _____

(meh-jee-koo)
Gostaria de chamar   um médico. _____
             call (as in summon)   doctor

(meh-oo)
Meu número é 526-05-29. _____
my

(seh-oo)
Qual é o seu   número? _____
what   your

Qual é o número do hotel? _____
            of the

Marília: Bom dia. Aqui é Marília Menezes. Gostaria de falar com o Senhor Torres.

_____

(oh-koo-pah-doo)
Secretária: Um momento. Desculpe, o telefone está ocupado.
                                                  busy / occupied

_____

(poh-jee) (heh-peh-cheer)
Marília: Pode repetir   por favor?
         can you

_____

Secretária: Desculpe, o telefone está ocupado.

_____

Marília: Está bem. Obrigada.

_____

Agora você are ready to use any **telefone**, anywhere. Just take it slowly **e** speak clearly.

❏ **a Cuba** *(koo-bah)* . . . . Cuba
❏ **o Equador** *(eh-kwah-dor)*. . . . . Ecuador   _____
❏ **a Espanha** *(es-pahn-yah)* . . . . Spain   _____
❏ **o México** *(meh-shee-koo)* . . . . Mexico   _____
❏ **o Moçambique** *(moh-sahm-bee-kee)* . . . . Mozambique   _____

(meh-troh)
"O metrô" é o nome português para "the subway." Há um metrô no Rio e em São Paulo.

Ônibus are also muito popular e let you see the sights as well, but they can be very full at certain

times of the day.

(meh-troh)
o metrô
subway

(ow-nee-boos)
o ônibus
bus

(es-tah-sown) *(meh-troh)*
a estação de metrô
station

(pohn-too)
o ponto de táxi
stop

(ow-nee-boos)
o ponto de ônibus

(leen-yahs) *(pah-rah-dahs)* *(es-tah-sown)*
Maps displaying the various **linhas** e **paradas** are generally posted inside every **estação**
lines stops station

de metrô. As linhas are generally color-coded to facilitate reading just like your example on the

(leen-yah)
next page. How do **você** use **o metrô?** Check **o nome** of the last **parada** on **a linha** which **você**

want to take **e** catch **o metrô** traveling in that direction.

❐	**o Panamá** *(pah-nah-mah)*	....	Panama	_____
❐	**o Paraguai** *(pah-rah-gwhy)*	....	Paraguay	_____
❐	**o Peru** *(peh-roo)*	....	Peru	_____
❐	**o Uruguai** *(oo-roo-gwhy)*	....	Uruguay	_____
❐	**a Venezuela** *(veh-neh-zoo-eh-lah)*	....	Venezuela	_____

Agora, locate your destination, select the correct line on your practice **metrô e** hop on board.

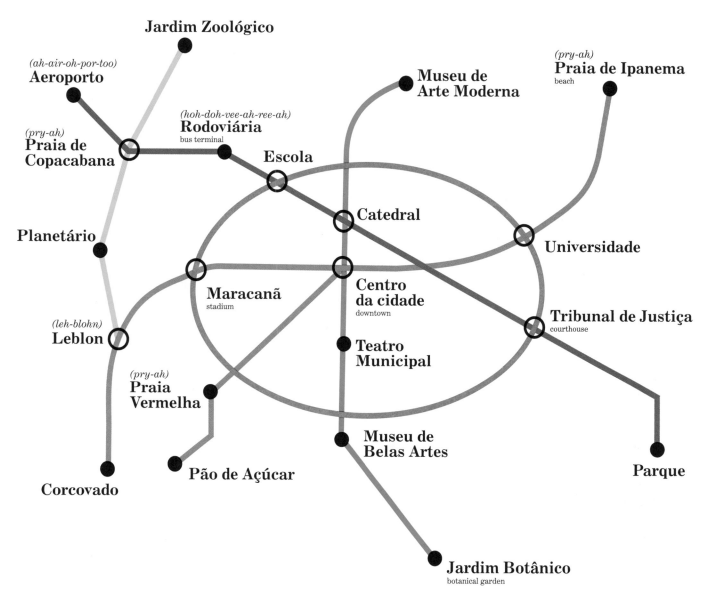

Say these questions aloud many times and don't forget your **passagem de metrô!**

(es-tah-sown)
Onde é a estação de metrô?

Onde é o ponto de ônibus?

Onde é o ponto de táxi?

metrô

Aqui are a few holidays **e** greetings which **você** might experience during your visit.
- **véspera de ano novo** *(vehs-peh-rah)(jee)(ah-noo)(noh-voo)* . . . . New Year's Eve (Dec. 31)
- **dia de ano novo** *(jee-ah)(jee)(ah-noo)(noh-voo)* . . . . New Year's Day (Jan. 1)
  – **Feliz Ano Novo!** *(feh-lees)(ah-noo)(noh-voo)* . . . . Happy New Year!
- **Feliz aniversário!** *(feh-lees)(ah-nee-vair-sah-ree-oo)* . . . . Happy Birthday!

Practice the following basic **perguntas** *(pair-goon-tahs)* out loud **e** then write them in the blanks below.

questions

1. **Com que freqüência vem o metrô?** *(freh-kwane-see-ah)* _____
    how often   comes

    Com que freqüência vem o ônibus? _____

    Com que freqüência vem o trem? _____

2. **A que horas vem o metrô?** _____

    A que horas vem o ônibus? _____ *A que horas vem o ônibus?* _____

    A que horas vem o trem? _____

3. **Quanto custa uma passagem de metrô?** _____

    Quanto custa uma passagem de ônibus? _____

    Quanto custa uma passagem de avião? _____

4. **Onde posso comprar uma passagem de metrô?** _____
    can (I) buy

    Onde posso comprar uma passagem de ônibus? _____

    Onde posso comprar uma passagem de avião? _____

Let's change directions **e** learn **três** new verbs. **Você** know the basic "plug-in" formula, so

write out your own sentences using these new verbs.

(lah-var)
lavar _____
to wash

(pair-dair)
perder _____
to lose

(toh-mar)
tomar _____
to take

❏ **Páscoa** *(pahs-koh-ah)* . . . . Easter
– **Feliz Páscoa!** *(feh-lees)(pahs-koh-ah)*. . . . . Happy Easter!
❏ **véspera de Natal** *(vehs-peh-rah)(jeh)(nah-tahl)* . . . . Christmas Eve (Dec. 24)
❏ **Natal** *(nah-tahl)* . . . . Christmas (Dec. 25)
– **Feliz Natal!** *(feh-lees)(nah-tahl)* . . . . Merry Christmas!

23

(vehn-dair) *(kohm-prar)*
Vender e Comprar
to sell   to buy

Shopping abroad is exciting. The simple everyday task of buying **um litro** *(lee-troo)* **de leite** *(lay-chee)* **ou uma**
liter   milk

(mah-sah)
maçã becomes a challenge that **você** should **agora** be able to meet quickly **e** easily. Of course,
apple

você will purchase **lembranças,** *(lame-brahn-sahs)* **selos** *(seh-loosh)* **e cartões** *(kar-toynsh)* **postais** *(pohs-tiesh)* but do not forget those many other
souvenirs

items ranging from shoelaces to **aspirina** *(ahs-pee-ree-nah)* that **você** might need unexpectedly. Locate your
aspirin

store, draw a line to it **e,** as always, write your new words in the blanks provided.

(mah-gah-zee-nee) *(grahn-jee)* *(ar-mah-zame)*
o magazine / o grande armazém
department store (Brazil)   department store (Portugal)

_____

(see-neh-mah)
o cinema _____
cinema

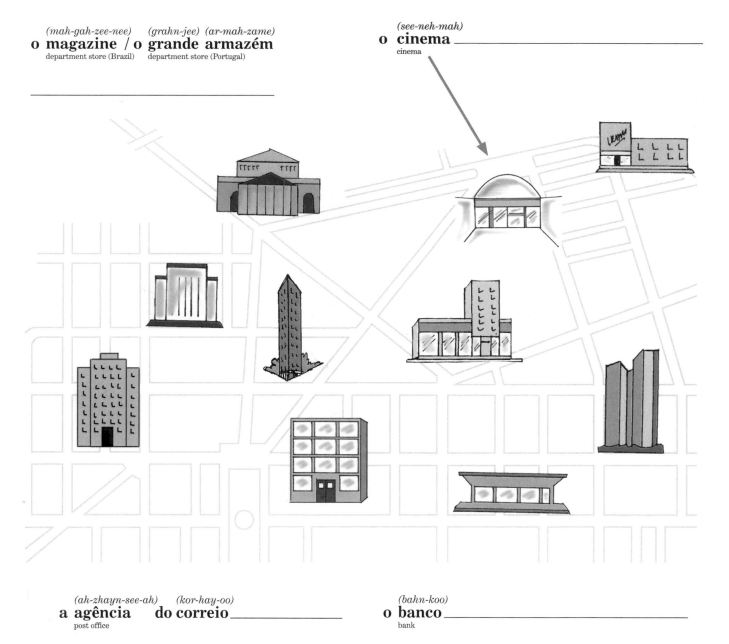

(ah-zhayn-see-ah) *(kor-hay-oo)*
a agência do correio_____
post office

(bahn-koo)
o banco_____
bank

(oh-tel) *(poh-zah-dah)*
o hotel / a pousada _____
hotel   inn

(pohs-too) *(jee)* *(gah-zoh-lee-nah)*
o posto de gasolina _____
service station

(cheen-too-rah-ree-ah)
a tinturaria
dry cleaners

(lee-vrah-ree-ah)
a livraria
bookstore

_____

_____

(loh-zhahs) *(ah-bair-tahs)*
As lojas estão generally **abertas** from
stores   open

8:00 or 8:30 until 19:00.

_____
(ah-soh-gee) *(tahl-yoo)*
o açougue / o talho
butcher shop (Brazil)   butcher shop (Portugal)

_____
(mair-kah-doo) *(froo-tahs)* *(leh-goo-meesh)*
o mercado de frutas e legumes
greengrocer

_____
(far-mah-see-ah)
a farmácia
pharmacy, drugstore

_____
(es-tah-see-oh-nah-mehn-too)
o estacionamento
parking lot

E

_____
(zhor-nah-lay-roo)
o jornaleiro
newsstand

_____
(ah-zhayn-see-ah) *(vee-ah-zhehns)*
a agência de viagens
travel agency

_____
(deh-leh-gah-see-ah) *(poh-lee-see-ah)*
a delegacia de polícia
police station

Sábados stores **estão** usually **abertas** until
                                          open

(may-oh-jee-ah)
meio-dia. Elas are **fechadas aos domingos.**
noon   closed

Shopping malls tend to be **abertas** on both

sábados e domingos.

(deh-lee-kah-tehs-sen)
a delicatessen
delicatessen

(shah-roo-tah-ree-ah)
a charutaria
tobacco shop

_____

_____

100

(bar-zeen-yoo)
o barzinho
beverage bar with snacks

_____

(floh-ree-kool-too-rah)
a floricultura
florist shop

_____

(pay-shah-ree-ah)
a peixaria _____
fish store

(loh-zhah) (mah-teh-ree-ahl) (foh-toh-grah-fee-koo)
a loja de material fotográfico _____
camera store

(mair-kah-doo)
o mercado _____
market

(soo-pair-mair-kah-doo)
o supermercado _____
supermarket

(heh-loh-zhoh-ah-ree-ah)
a relojoaria _____
watchmaker's shop

(pah-dah-ree-ah)
a padaria ___ *a padaria, a padaria* ___
bakery

(loh-zhah) (doh-seesh)
a loja de doces _____
pastry shop

(lah-vahn-deh-ree-ah)
a lavanderia _____
laundry

Nos Estados Unidos, the ground floor **e** the

first floor are one and the same. **No Brasil**

(tair-heh-oo)
the ground floor is called **o térreo** (**T**). The

(pree-may-roo) (pee-zoo)
primeiro piso (1° piso) é the next floor up **e**
first   floor

so on.

(pah-peh-lah-ree-ah)
a papelaria
stationery store

_____

(kah-beh-lay-ray-roo)
o cabeleireiro
hairdresser

_____

101

At this point, **você** should just about be ready for your **viagem.** **Você** have gone shopping for

those last-minute odds 'n ends. Most likely, the store directory at your local **magine** *(mah-gah-zee-nee)* did not
department store

look like the one **abaixo!** *(ah-by-shoo)* **"Criança"** *(kree-ahn-sah)* is Portuguese for "<u>child</u>" so if **você precisa de** something
need

for a child, **você** would probably look on **terçeiro piso, não é?** *(tair-say-roo)*

4º PISO	iluminação artigos para bebês seção de perdidos	serviços ao cliente cerâmicas porcelana	móveis antiguidades acessórios para carros

3º PISO	vestuário
	   feminino
	tudo para crianças
		vestuário
		   masculino
		artigos esportivos
		brinquedos
			artigos para
			   presente
			roupa de cama
			quadros

2º PISO	alimentação doces charutaria café	bebidas jornais e revistas discos	móveis de escritório artigos de cozinha

1º PISO	ternos masculinos
	sapatos de homem
	instrumentos
	   musicais
		bolsas e malas
		eletrônicos
		artigos de
		   informática
			livros
			jóias e bijuterias
			papelaria

T	máquina fotográfica guarda-chuvas relógios	vídeos perucas artigos de praia chapéus femininos	roupas íntimas perfumaria sapatos femininos

Let's start a checklist **para a sua viagem.** *(vee-ah-zhame)* Besides **roupas, o que você precisa?** *(hoh-pahs)* As you learn
your   clothing

these **palavras,** assemble these items **em um canto** *(kahn-too)* of your **casa.** Check **e** make sure that they
corner

estão limpas e *(leem-pahs)* ready **para a sua viagem.** Be sure to do the same **com** the rest of **as coisas** *(koy-zahs)*
clean

that **você** pack. On the next pages, match each item to its picture, draw a line to it and write out

the word many times. As **você** organize these things, check them off on this list. Do not forget to

take the next group of sticky labels and label these **coisas hoje.** *(koy-zahs)*
today

(pahs-sah-por-chee)
o passaporte
passport

(mah-lah)
a mala
suitcase

(pahs-sah-zhame) *(ah-vee-own)*
a passagem de avião
ticket

(bohl-sah)
a bolsa
handbag

a bolsa, a bolsa, a bolsa ✔

(kar-tay-rah)
a carteira
wallet

(jeen-yay-roo)
o dinheiro
money

(kar-toynsh) *(kreh-jee-too)*
os cartões de crédito
credit cards

(sheck-esh) *(vee-ah-zhame)*
os cheques de viagem
traveler's checks

(mah-key-nah) *(foh-toh-grah-fee-kah)*
a máquina fotográfica
camera

(feel-mee)
o filme
film

(soon-gah)
a sunga
swimsuit (♂)

(my-oh)
o maiô
swimsuit (♀)

(sahn-dah-lee-ahs)
as sandálias
sandals

(oh-koo-loosh) *(sohl)*
os óculos de sol
sunglasses

(es-koh-vah) *(dehn-chees)*
a escova de dentes
toothbrush

(pahs-tah) *(dehn-chees)*
a pasta de dentes
toothpaste

(sah-boh-neh-chee)
o sabonete
soap

(ah-pah-rel-yoo) *(bar-beh-ar)*
o aparelho de barbear
razor

(deh-zoh-doh-rahn-chee)
o desodorante
deodorant

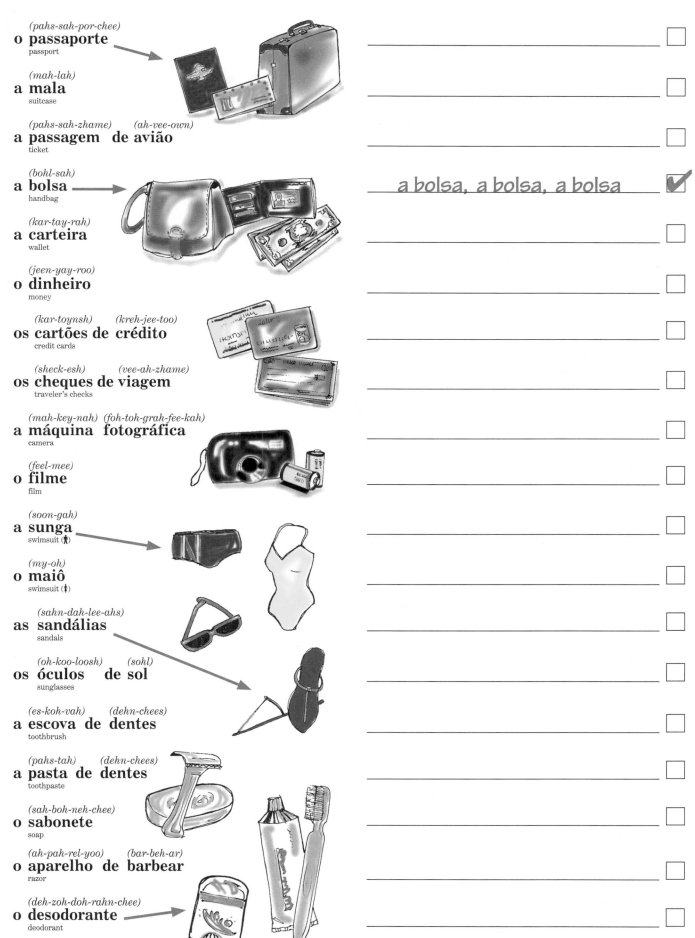

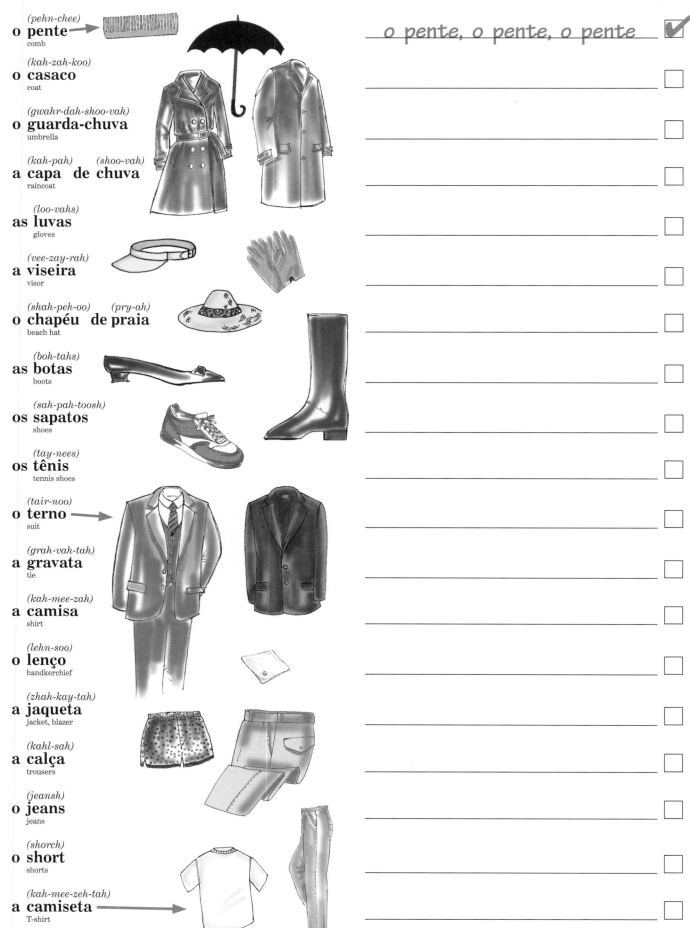

(pehn-chee)
o pente
comb

o pente, o pente, o pente ✓

(kah-zah-koo)
o casaco
coat

(gwahr-dah-shoo-vah)
o guarda-chuva
umbrella

(kah-pah) *(shoo-vah)*
a capa de chuva
raincoat

(loo-vahs)
as luvas
gloves

(vee-zay-rah)
a viseira
visor

(shah-peh-oo) *(pry-ah)*
o chapéu de praia
beach hat

(boh-tahs)
as botas
boots

(sah-pah-toosh)
os sapatos
shoes

(tay-nees)
os tênis
tennis shoes

(tair-noo)
o terno
suit

(grah-vah-tah)
a gravata
tie

(kah-mee-zah)
a camisa
shirt

(lehn-soo)
o lenço
handkerchief

(zhah-kay-tah)
a jaqueta
jacket, blazer

(kahl-sah)
a calça
trousers

(jeansh)
o jeans
jeans

(shorch)
o short
shorts

(kah-mee-zeh-tah)
a camiseta
T-shirt

(koo-eh-kah)
a cueca
underpants

_____ ☐

(kah-mee-zeh-tah)
a camiseta
undershirt

_____ ☐

(vehs-chee-doo)
o vestido
dress

_____ ☐

(bloo-zah)
a blusa
blouse

_____ ☐

(sy-ah)
a saia
skirt

a saia, a saia, a saia, a saia ✔

(soo-eh-tair)
a suéter
sweater

_____ ☐

(kohm-bee-nah-sown)
a combinação
slip

_____ ☐

(soo-chee-own)
o sutiã
bra

_____ ☐

(kahl-seen-yah)
a calcinha
underpants

_____ ☐

(may-ahs)
as meias
socks

_____ ☐

(may-ah-kahl-sah)
a meia-calça
pantyhose

_____ ☐

(pee-zhah-mah)
o pijama
pajamas

_____ ☐

(kah-mee-zoh-lah)
a camisola
nightshirt

_____ ☐

(hoh-pown) *(bahn-yoo)*
o roupão de banho
bathrobe

_____ ☐

(shee-neh-loosh)
os chinelos
slippers

_____ ☐

From now on, **você tem "sabonete"** *(sah-boh-neh-chee)* **e não** "soap." Having assembled these *(koy-zahs)* **coisas, você** are
                                                                                                                    things
ready **para viajar.** Let's add these important shopping phrases to your basic repertoire.

(kay) (tah-mahn-yoo)
Que tamanho? _____
what   size

(es-chee) (vehs-chee)   *(sair-vee)*
Este veste bem. / Este serve bem. _____
this   fits   well   fits

(vehs-chee)
Este não veste bem. / Este não serve bem. _____
           does not fit

Treat yourself to a final review. **Você sabe** the names for **lojas** *(loh-zhahs)* **em português,** so let's practice shopping. Just remember your key question **palavras** that you learned in Step 2. Whether **você** need to buy **bolsas ou livros** the necessary **palavras** are the same.

1.   First step — **onde?**

Onde é a padaria?   **Onde é o banco?**   **Onde é o jornaleiro?** *(zhor-nah-lay-roo)*

_____

(Where is the department store?)

_____

(Where is the market?)

_____

(Where is the supermarket?)

2.   Second step — tell them what **você** are looking for, **precisa ou quer!**

Eu preciso de . . . *(preh-see-zoo) (dee)*   **Eu quero . . .**   **Você tem . . . ?**
need   want   do you have

_____

(Do you have postcards?)

_____

(I want four stamps.)

_____

(I need toothpaste.)

_____

(I want to buy film.)

_____

(Do you have coffee?)

Go through the glossary at the end of this **livro e** select **vinte** *(veen-chee)* **palavras.** Drill the above

patterns **com** these twenty **palavras.** Don't cheat. Drill them **hoje. Agora,** take **vinte** more

palavras do your glossary **e** do the same.
_{from}

3. Third step — find out **quanto custa a coisa.** *(koos-tah)* *(koy-zah)*

Quanto custa isso?   **Quanto custa um litro de leite?** *(lay-chee)*   **Quanto custa um selo?**
_{liter   milk}

(How much does the toothpaste cost?)

(How much does the soap cost?)

(How much does a cup of tea cost?)

4.   Fourth step — success! I found it!

Once **você** find what **você** would like, **diga,** *(jee-gah)*
_{say}

Quero este, por favor. *(es-chee)*
_{this one}

or

Me dá este, por favor.   *Me dá este, por favor.*
_{give me}

Ou if **você** would not like it, **diga,** *(jee-gah)*

Não quero este, obrigado.

or

Eu não gosto. *(gohs-too)*
_{I do not like it}

Congratulations! You have finished. By now you should have stuck your labels, flashed your

cards, cut out your menu guide and packed your **malas.** *(mah-lahs)* **Você** should be very pleased with your
_{suitcases}

accomplishment. You have learned what it sometimes takes others years to achieve and **você**

hopefully had fun doing it. **Boa viagem!**

Glossary

This glossary contains words used in this book only. It is not meant to be a dictionary. Consider purchasing a dictionary which best suits your needs—small for traveling, large for reference, or specialized for specific vocabulary needs.

Remember that Portuguese words can change their endings depending upon how they are used. Not all variations are given here, but in many cases you will see "o/a" at the end of a word. This should help you to remember that this word can change its ending. Learn to look for the core of the word.

A

a *(ah)* .... the
à cobrar *(ah)(koh-brar)* .... collect (telephone call)
à milanesa *(ah)(mee-lah-neh-zah)* ...... cooked in a batter
A que horas? *(ah)(kay)(oh-rahs)* .... At what time?
abaixo *(ah-by-shoo)* .... below
abajur, o *(ah-bah-zhoor)* .... lamp
aberto/a *(ah-bair-too)* .... open
abra *(ah-brah)* .... open!
abre *(ah-bree)* .... opens
abril *(ah-breel)* .... April
abrir *(ah-breer)* .... to open
absoluto/a *(ahb-soh-loo-too)* .... absolute
absurdo/a *(ahb-soor-doo)* .... absurd
acessórios para carros, os *(ah-sehs-soh-ree-oosh)(pah-rah)* . *(kar-hoosh)* .... automobile accessories
acidente, o *(ah-see-dehn-chee)* .... accident
açougue, o *(ah-soh-gee)* .... butcher shop
açúcar, o *(ah-soo-kar)* .... sugar
adeus *(ah-deh-oos)* .... good-bye
aeroporto, o *(ah-air-oh-por-too)* .... airport
África do Sul, a *(ah-free-kah)(doo)(sool)* ...... South Africa
agência de câmbio, a *(ah-zhayn-see-ah)(jeh)(kahm-bee-oo)* . ... money-exchange office
agência de viagens, a *(ah-zhayn-see-ah)(jeh)(vee-ah-zhehns)* .... travel agency
agência do correio, a *(ah-zhayn-see-ah)(doh)(kor-hay-oo)* .. .. post office
agora *(ah-goh-rah)* .... now
agosto *(ah-gohs-too)* .... August
agrião, o *(ah-gree-own)* .... watercress
água, a *(ah-gwah)* .... water
água com gás, a *(ah-gwah)(kohm)(gahz)* .. sparkling water
água mineral, a *(ah-gwah)(mee-neh-rahl)* ... mineral water
água tônica, a *(ah-gwah)(toh-nee-kah)* .... tonic water
álcool, o *(ahl-kohl)* .... alcohol
Alemanha, a *(ah-leh-mahn-yah)* .... Germany
alemão/a *(ah-leh-mown)* .... German
alfândega, a *(ahl-fane-deh-gah)* .... customs
ali *(ah-lee)* .... there
alimentação, a *(ah-lee-mehn-tah-sown)* .... food
almoço, o *(ahl-moh-soo)* .... lunch
alô *(ah-loh)* .... hello
alto/a *(ahl-too)* .... tall, high
aluguél de carros, o *(ah-loo-gehl)(jee)(kar-hoosh)* .... car-rental agency
amanhã *(ah-mahn-yahn)* .... tomorrow
amarelo/a *(ah-mah-reh-loo)* .... yellow
América, a *(ah-meh-ree-kah)* .... America
América do Norte, a *(ah-meh-ree-kah)(doo)(nor-chee)* .... North America
América do Sul, a *(ah-meh-ree-kah)(doo)(sool)* .... South America
americana, a *(ah-meh-ree-kah-nah)* .... American (♀)
americano, o *(ah-meh-ree-kah-noo)* .... American (♂)
amigo, o *(ah-mee-goo)* .... friend (male)
andar *(ahn-dar)* .... to walk
animal, o *(ah-nee-mahl)* .... animal
ano, o *(ah-noo)* .... year

antiguidades, as *(ahn-chee-gwee-dah-jeesh)* .... antiques
anual *(ah-noo-ahl)* .... annual
ao *(ah-oh)* .... to the
ao forno *(ah-oh)(for-noo)* .... baked
aos *(ah-ohs)* .... on the
aparelho de barbear, o *(ah-pah-rel-yoo)(deh)(bar-beh-ar)* ... . razor
apartamento, o *(ah-par-tah-mehn-too)* .... hotel room
aplicação, a *(ah-plee-kah-sown)* .... application
aprender *(ah-prehn-dair)* .... to learn
aproximadamente *(ah-proh-see-mah-dah-mehn-chee)* .... approximately
aqui *(ah-key)* .... here
Argentina, a *(ar-zhehn-chee-nah)* .... Argentina
armário, o *(ar-mah-ree-oo)* .... cupboard, wardrobe
arte, a *(ar-chee)* .... art
artesanato, o *(ar-teh-zah-nah-too)* .... crafts
artigos, os *(ar-chee-goosh)* .... goods, appliances
artigos de informática, os *(ar-chee-goosh)(jee)(een-for-mah-chee-kah)* .... computer goods
artista, a/o *(ar-chees-tah)* .... artist
as *(ahs)* .... the (plural, feminine)
às *(ahs)* .... at
aspirina, a *(ahs-pee-ree-nah)* .... aspirin
assado/a *(ahs-sah-doo)* .... roasted
assento, o *(ahs-sehn-too)* .... seat
assinatura, a *(ahs-see-nah-too-rah)* .... signature
até amanhã *(ah-teh)(ah-mahn-yahn)* ...... until tomorrow
até logo *(ah-teh)(loh-goo)* .... until then
atenção, a *(ah-tehn-sown)* .... attention
ativo *(ah-chee-voo)* .... active
atlântico/a *(aht-lahn-chee-koo)* .... Atlantic
ato, o *(ah-too)* .... act (of a play)
atrás *(ah-trahs)* .... behind
atum, o *(ah-toom)* .... tuna
Austrália, a *(ows-trah-lee-ah)* .... Australia
auto-estrada, a *(ow-too-es-trah-dah)* .... freeway
ave, a *(ah-vee)* .... bird
avenida, a *(ah-veh-nee-dah)* .... avenue
aves, as *(ah-veesh)* .... poultry
avião, o *(ah-vee-own)* .... airplane
avó, a *(ah-voh)* .... grandmother
avô, o *(ah-voh)* .... grandfather
azul *(ah-zool)* .... blue
azulejos pintados à mão, os *(ah-zoo-leh-zhoosh)(peen-tah-doosh)(ah)(mown)* .... hand-painted tiles

B

baixo/a *(by-shoo)* .... short, low
balão, o *(bah-lown)* .... balloon
balcão, o *(bahl-kown)* .... balcony, counter
balé, o *(bah-lay)* .... ballet
banco, o *(bahn-koo)* .... bank
banheiro, o *(bahn-yay-roo)* ...... restroom, bathroom
barato/a *(bah-rah-too)* .... inexpensive
barco, o *(bar-koo)* .... boat
barzinho, o *(bar-zeen-yoo)* .... street bar with snacks
básico/a *(bah-zee-koo)* .... basic
batata, a *(bah-tah-tah)* .... potato
bebê, o *(beh-bay)* .... baby

beber *(beh-bair)* . . . . to drink
bebida, a *(beh-bee-dah)* . . . . beverage
belas artes, as *(beh-lahs)(ar-chees)* . . . . fine arts
Bélgica, a *(bel-zhee-kah)* . . . . Belgium
bem *(bame)* . . . . well, good
bicicleta, a *(bee-see-kleh-tah)* . . . . bicycle
bife, o *(bee-fee)* . . . . beefsteak
bijuteria, a *(bee-zhoo-teh-ree-ah)* . . . . jewelry
biscoito, o *(bees-koy-too)* . . . . cookie
blusa, a *(bloo-zah)* . . . . blouse
boa noite *(boh-ah)(noy-chee)* . . . . good night
boa sorte *(boh-ah)(sor-chee)* . . . . good luck
boa tarde *(boh-ah)(tar-jee)* . . . . good afternoon
Boa viagem! *(boh-ah)(vee-ah-zhame)* . . . . . Have a good trip!
Bolívia, a *(boh-lee-vee-ah)* . . . . Bolivia
bolo, o *(boh-loo)* . . . . .cake
bolsa, a *(bohl-sah)* . . . . handbag
bom *(bohm)* . . . . good
Bom apetite! *(bohm)(ah-peh-chee-chee)* . . Enjoy your meal!
bom dia *(bohm)(jee-ah)* . . . . . . good morning, good day, hello
botas, as *(boh-tahs)* . . . . boots
branco *(brahn-koo)* . . . . white
Brasil, o *(brah-zeel)* . . . . Brazil
brasileiro/a *(brah-zee-lay-roo)* . . . . Brazilian
brinquedos, os *(breen-kay-doosh)* . . . . toys

C

cabeleireiro, o *(kah-beh-lay-ray-roo)* . . . . hairdresser
cabine telefônica, a *(kah-bee-nee)(teh-leh-foh-nee-kah)* . . . . .
. . . . telephone booth
cachorro, o *(kah-shor-hoo)* . . . . dog
cadeira, a *(kah-day-rah)* . . . . chair
café da manhã, o *(kah-fay)(dah)(mahn-yahn)* . . . breakfast
café, o *(kah-fay)* . . . . coffee, coffee house, coffee shop
cafezinho, o *(kah-fay-zeen-yoo)* . . . . . . espresso-type coffee
caixa do correio, a *(ky-shah)(doh)(kor-hay-oo)* . . . . mailbox
caixa, o/a *(ky-shah)* . . . . cashier
caju, o *(kah-zhoo)* . . . . cashew fruit
calça, a *(kahl-sah)* . . . . trousers
calcinha, a *(kahl-seen-yah)* . . . . underpants (♀)
calendário, o *(kah-lehn-dah-ree-oo)* . . . . calendar
calma, a *(kahl-mah)* . . . . calm
calor, o *(kah-lor)* . . . . heat
cama, a *(kah-mah)* . . . . bed
camisa, a *(kah-mee-zah)* . . . . shirt
camiseta, a *(kah-mee-zeh-tah)* . . . . T-shirt, undershirt
camisola, a *(kah-mee-zoh-lah)* . . . . nightshirt
Canadá, o *(kah-nah-dah)* . . . . Canada
canadense *(kah-nah-dehn-see)* . . . . Canadian
caneta, a *(kah-neh-tah)* . . . . pen
canto, o *(kahn-too)* . . . . corner
cão, o *(kown)* . . . . dog
capa de chuva, a *(kah-pah)(jeh)(shoo-vah)* . . . . raincoat
capacidade, a *(kah-pah-see-dah-jee)* . . . . capacity
capela, a *(kah-peh-lah)* . . . . chapel
capital, a *(kah-pee-tahl)* . . . . capital
caramelo, o *(kah-rah-meh-loo)* . . . . caramel
caranguejo, o *(kah-rahn-gay-zhoo)* . . . . crab
cardápio, o *(kar-dah-pee-oo)* . . . . menu
Carnaval, o *(kar-nah-vahl)* . . . . carnival
carne, a *(kar-nee)* . . . . meat
carneiro, o *(kar-nay-roo)* . . . . mutton
caro/a *(kah-roo)* . . . . expensive
carregador, o *(kar-heh-gah-dor)* . . . . porter
carro, o *(kar-hoo)* . . . . car
carro alugado, o *(kar-hoo)(ah-loo-gah-doo)* . . . . . rental car
carta, a *(kar-tah)* . . . . letter
cartão de telefone, o *(kar-town)(jee)(teh-leh-foh-nee)* . . . . . .
. . . . phonecard
cartão postal, o *(kar-town)(pohs-tahl)* . . . . postcard
cartão SIM, o *(kar-town)(seem)* . . . . SIM card
carteira, a *(kar-tay-rah)* . . . . wallet
cartões de crédito, os *(kar-toynsh)(jeh)(kreh-jee-too)* . . . . . .
. . . . credit cards
casa, a *(kah-zah)* . . . . house

casaco, o *(kah-zah-koo)* . . . . coat
catedral, a *(kah-teh-drahl)* . . . . cathedral
católico/a *(kah-toh-lee-koo)* . . . . Catholic
catorze *(kah-tor-zee)* . . . . fourteen
causa, a *(kow-zah)* . . . . cause
cavalheiro, o *(kah-vahl-yay-roo)* . . . . man
cem *(same)* . . . . one hundred
centígrado, o *(sehn-chee-grah-doo)* . . . . Centigrade
centro, o *(sehn-troo)* . . . . center
cerâmica, a *(seh-rah-mee-kah)* . . . . ceramics
cerveja, a *(sair-veh-zhah)* . . . . beer
cesto de papel, o *(sehs-too)(jeh)(pah-pel)* . . wastepaper basket
chá, o *(shah)* . . . . tea
chá mate, o *(shah)(mah-chee)* . . . . Brazilian iced tea
chamada, a *(shah-mah-dah)* . . . . call, telephone call
chamar *(shah-mar)* . . . . to call
champanhe, a/o *(shahm-pahn-yee)* . . . . champagne
chapéu de praia, o *(shah-peh-oo)(jee)(pry-ah)* . . . . beach hat
charutaria, a *(shah-roo-tah-ree-ah)* . . . . tobacco shop
chegada, a *(sheh-gah-dah)* . . . . arrival
chegar *(sheh-gar)* . . . . to arrive
cheque, o *(sheck-ee)* . . . . check
cheques de viagem, os *(sheck-esh)(jeh)(vee-ah-zhame)* . . . . .
. . . . traveler's checks
Chile, o *(shee-lee)* . . . . Chile
chinelos, os *(shee-neh-loosh)* . . . . slippers
chinês *(shee-naysh)* . . . . Chinese
chocolate quente, o *(shoh-koh-lah-chee)(kane-chee)* . . . . . .
. . . . hot chocolate
chocolate, o *(shoh-koh-lah-chee)* . . . . chocolate
chope, o *(shoh-pee)* . . . . draught beer
chove *(shoh-vee)* . . . . it rains
churrasco, o *(shoor-hahs-koo)* . . . . barbecue
chuveiro, o *(shoo-vay-roo)* . . . . shower
cidade, a *(see-dah-jee)* . . . . city
científico *(see-ehn-chee-fee-koo)* . . . . scientific
cinco *(seen-koo)* . . . . five
cinema, o *(see-neh-mah)* . . . . cinema
cinqüenta *(seen-kwehn-tah)* . . . . fifty
cinza *(seen-zah)* . . . . gray
clássico/a *(klahs-see-koo)* . . . . classical, classic
closet, o *(kloh-zet)* . . . . closet
cobertor, o *(koh-bair-tor)* . . . . blanket
coisa, a *(koy-zah)* . . . . thing
colher, a *(kohl-yair)* . . . . spoon
Colômbia, a *(koh-lohm-bee-ah)* . . . . Colombia
com *(kohm)* . . . . .with
com fome *(kohm)(foh-mee)* . . . . with hunger
com licença *(kohm)(lee-sehn-sah)* . . . . excuse me
com sede *(kohm)(seh-jee)* . . . . with thirst
combinação, a *(kohm-bee-nah-sown)* . . . . slip
começar *(koh-meh-sar)* . . . . to begin, to commence
comer *(koh-mair)* . . . . to eat
cômico/a *(koh-mee-koo)* . . . . comical
como *(koh-moo)* . . . . how
Como vai? *(koh-moo)(vy)* . . . . How are you?
companhia, a *(kohm-pahn-yee-ah)* . . . . company
complicado/a *(kohm-plee-kah-doo)* . . . . complicated
comprar *(kohm-prar)* . . . . to buy
computador, o *(kohm-poo-tah-dor)* . . . . computer
concerto, o *(kohn-sair-too)* . . . . concert
conhaque, o *(kohn-yah-kay)* . . . . cognac, brandy
conta, a *(kohn-tah)* . . . . bill
conversação, a *(kohn-vair-sah-sown)* . . . . conversation
conversação telefônica, a *(kohn-vair-sah-sown)(teh-leh-foh-nee-kah)* . . . . telephone conversation
cópia, a *(koh-pee-ah)* . . . . copy
copo de vinho, o *(koh-poo)(jee)(veen-yoo)* . . . . . . wine glass
copo, o *(koh-poo)* . . . . glass
cor, a *(kor)* . . . . color
Corcovado, o *(kor-koh-vah-doo)* . . . . mountain in Rio
cordeiro, o *(kor-day-roo)* . . . . lamb
corredor, o *(kor-heh-dor)* . . . . aisle
correio, o *(koh-hay-oo)* . . . . mail, post office

correspondência, a *(kor-hehs-pohn-dane-see-ah)* ..... mail
correto/a *(kor-heh-too)* .... correct
cortina, a *(kor-chee-nah)* .... curtain
costa, a *(kohs-tah)* .... coast
Costa Rica, a *(kohs-tah)(hee-kah)* .... Costa Rica
couro, o *(koh-roo)* .... leather
cozido/a *(koh-zee-doo)* .... cooked
cozido no vapor *(koh-zee-doo)(noh)(vah-por)* ..... steamed
cozinha, a *(koh-zeen-yah)* .... kitchen
creme, o *(kreh-mee)* .... cream
criança, a *(kree-ahn-sah)* .... child
Cristo Redentor *(krees-too)(heh-dehn-tor)* ....
.... Christ, the Redeemer
Cuba, a *(koo-bah)* .... Cuba
cueca, a *(koo-eh-kah)* .... underpants (male)
cultura, a *(kool-too-rah)* .... culture
curto/a *(koor-too)* .... short
custa *(koos-tah)* .... (it) costs
custar *(koos-tar)* .... to cost

D

da (de + a) *(dah)* .... from the, of the
dama, a *(dah-mah)* .... woman
da-me *(dah-mee)* .... give me (Portugal)
de *(deh), (jee), (dee), (jeh)* .... of, from
de ida *(jee)(ee-dah)* .... one way
de ida e volta *(jee)(ee-dah)(eh)(vohl-tah)* .... round trip
de nada *(jee)(nah-dah)* .... you're welcome
decisão, a *(deh-see-sown)* .... decision
declaração, a *(deh-klah-rah-sown)* .... declaration
delegacia de polícia, a *(deh-leh-gah-see-ah)(deh)*
   (poh-lee-see-ah) .... police station
delicatessen, a *(deh-lee-kah-tehs-sen)* ...... delicatessen
delicioso/a *(deh-lee-see-oh-zoo)* .... delicious
desconforto, o *(dehs-kohn-for-too)* .... discomfort
desculpe *(dehs-kool-pee)* ...... excuse me (as in I am sorry)
desodorante, o *(deh-zoh-doh-rahn-chee)* .... deodorant
despertador, o *(dehs-pair-tah-dor)* .... alarm clock
desvio, o *(dehs-vee-oo)* .... detour
devagar *(deh-vah-gar)* .... slow
dez *(dehsh)* .... ten
dezembro *(deh-zem-broo)* .... December
dezenove *(deh-zeh-noh-vee)* .... nineteen
dezesseis *(deh-zehs-saysh)* .... sixteen
dezessete *(deh-zehs-seh-chee)* .... seventeen
dezoito *(deh-zoy-too)* .... eighteen
dia, o *(jee-ah)* .... day
dia de ano novo, o *(jee-ah)(jee)(ah-noo)(noh-voo)* ....
.... New Year's Day
dicionário, o *(jee-see-oh-nah-ree-oo)* .... dictionary
diferença, a *(jee-feh-rehn-sah)* .... difference
diferente *(jee-feh-rehn-chee)* .... different
difícil *(jee-fee-seel)* .... difficult
diga *(jee-gah)* .... say!
dinheiro, o *(jeen-yay-roo)* .... money
direção, a *(jee-reh-sown)* .... direction
direita *(jee-ray-tah)* .... right
disco, o *(jees-koo)* .... disc, record, CD
discreto *(jees-kreh-too)* .... discreet
distância, a *(jees-tahn-see-ah)* .... distance
divisão, a *(jee-vee-sown)* .... division
dizer *(jee-zair)* .... to say
do (de + o) *(doo), (doh)* .... from the, of the
do lado de *(doo)(lah-doo)(dee)* .... next to
doce, o *(doh-see)* .... pastry
documento, o *(doh-koo-mehn-too)* .... document
doente *(doh-ehn-chee)* .... sick
dois *(doysh)* .... two
dólar, o *(doh-lar)* .... dollar
doméstico/a *(doh-mehs-chee-koo)* .... domestic
domingo, o *(doh-meen-goo)* .... Sunday
dona, a *(doh-nah)* ...... lady, housewife (term of respect)
dormir *(dor-meer)* .... to sleep
dos *(dohs)* .... from the

doutor, o *(doh-tor)* .... doctor (title)
doze *(doh-zee)* .... twelve
duas *(doo-ahs)* .... two

E

é *(eh)* .... is, (it) is
e *(eh)* .... and
e meia *(eh)(may-ah)* .... half past
E para beber? *(eh)(pah-rah)(beh-bair)* ...... And to drink?
economia, a *(eh-koh-noh-mee-ah)* .... economy
Ecuador, o *(eh-kwah-dor)* .... Ecuador
ela *(eh-lah)* .... she
elas *(eh-lahs)* .... they (♀)
ele *(eh-lee)* .... he
eles *(eh-leesh)* .... they (♂ or mixed)
elétrico/a *(eh-leh-tree-koo)* .... electric
eletrônicos, os *(eh-leh-troh-nee-koosh)* .... electronic goods
em *(ehm)* .... in, into
em cima *(ehm)(see-mah)* .... upstairs, on top
em frente *(ehm)(frehn-chee)* .... straight ahead
em frente de *(ehm)(frehn-chee)(dee)* .... in front of
e-mail, o *(ee-may-oo)* .... email
embaixo *(ehm-by shoo)* .... downstairs
embaixo de *(ehm-by-shoo)(dee)* .... under
empurre *(ehm-poor-hee)* .... push! (doors)
encomenda, a *(ehn-koh-mehn-dah)* .... order
encontrar *(ehn-kohn-trar)* .... to find, to meet
endereço, o *(ehn-deh-reh-soo)* .... address
enorme *(eh-nor-mee)* .... enormous
entender *(ehn-tehn-dair)* .... to understand
entrada, a *(ehn-trah-dah)* .... entrance, main course
entrar *(ehn-trar)* .... to enter
entre *(ehn-tree)* .... between
erro, o *(air-hoo)* .... error
escola, a *(es-koh-lah)* .... school
escova de dentes, a *(es-koh-vah)(jee)(dehn-chees)* .toothbrush
escreva *(es-kreh-vah)* .... write!, write out!
escrever *(es-kreh-vair)* .... to write
escritório, o *(es-kree-toh-ree-oo)* .... office
espaço, o *(es-pah-soo)* .... space
Espanha, a *(es-pahn-yah)* .... Spain
espanhol *(es-pahn-yohl)* .... Spanish
especial do dia, o *(es-peh-see-ahl)(doo)(jee-ah)* . .daily special
espelho, o *(es-pel-yoo)* .... mirror
esplêndido *(es-plehn-jee-doo)* .... splendid
esporte, o *(es-por-chee)* .... sport
esquerda *(es-kair-dah)* .... left
está *(es-tah)* .... is
estabilidade, a *(es-tah-bee-lee-dah-jee)* .... stability
estação, a *(es-tah-sown)* .... station
estação de metrô, a *(es-tah-sown)(jee)(meh-troh)* ....
.... subway station
estação de trem, a *(es-tah-sown)(jee)(trame)* .. train station
estacionamento, o *(es-tah-see-oh-nah-mehn-too)* . parking lot
estacionar *(es-tah-see-oh-nar)* .... to park
estado, o *(es-tah-doo)* .... state
Estados Unidos, os *(es-tah-doosh)(oo-nee-doosh)* ....
.... the United States
estão *(es-town)* .... (they) are
estas *(es-tahs)* .... these
estátua, a *(es-tah-too-ah)* .... statue
estava *(es-tah-vah)* .... (it) was
este *(es-chee)* .... this, this one
estou *(es-toh)* .... (I) am
estrada, a *(es-trah-dah)* .... road
estudante, a/o *(es-too-dahn-chee)* .... student
eu *(eh-oo)* I
eu estou *(eh-oo)(es-toh)* .... I am
eu quero *(eh-oo)(kair-oo)* .... I want
eu sou *(eh-oo)(soh)* .... I am
eu tenho *(eh-oo)(tehn-yoo)* .... I have
Europa, a *(eh-oo-roh-pah)* .... Europe
exato/a *(eh-zah-too)* .... exact
excelente *(eh-seh-lehn-chee)* .... excellent

exemplo, o *(eh-zame-ploo)* .... example
experiência, a *(es-peh-ree-ayn-see-ah)* .... experience
expressão, a *(es-prehs-sown)* .... expression
extremo,o *(es-treh-moo)* .... extreme

F

faca, a *(fah-kah)* .... knife
fahrenheit *(fah-rehn-heit)* .... Fahrenheit
falar *(fah-lar)* .... to speak
fama, a *(fah-mah)* .... fame
família, a *(fah-mee-lee-ah)* .... family
famoso/a *(fah-moh-zoo)* .... famous
farmácia, a *(far-mah-see-ah)* .... pharmacy, drugstore
favor, o *(fah-vor)* .... favor
fax, o *(fahks)* .... fax
faz *(fahs)* .... it makes
fazer *(fah-zair)* .... to make, to do
fazer a mala *(fah-zair)(ah)(mah-lah)* .... to pack
fechado/a *(feh-shah-doo)* .... closed
fechar *(feh-shar)* .... to close
feira, a *(fay-rah)* .... market
feito/a *(fay-too)* .... finished, ready
Feliz Aniversário! *(feh-lees)(ah-nee-vair-sah-ree-oo)* ....
.... Happy Birthday
Feliz Ano Novo! *(feh-lees)(ah-noo)(noh-voo)* Happy New Year
Feliz Natal! *(feh-lees)(nah-tahl)* .... Merry Christmas
Feliz Páscoa! *(feh-lees)(pahs-koh-ah)* ..... Happy Easter
festival, o *(fehs-chee-vahl)* .... festival
fevereiro *(feh-veh-ray-roo)* .... February
figura, a *(fee-goo-rah)* .... figure
filé, o *(fee-lay)* .... filet
filha, a *(feel-yah)* .... daughter
filho, o *(feel-yoo)* .... son
filhos, os *(feel-yoosh)* .... children
filme, o *(feel-mee)* .... film
final, o *(fee-nahl)* .... final
flor, a *(flor)* .... flower
floricultura, a *(floh-ree-kool-too-rah)* .... florist shop
fogão, o *(foh-gown)* .... stove
foi *(foy)* .... was
folclore, o *(fohl-kloh-ree)* .... folklore
fome, a *(foh-mee)* .... hunger
forma, a *(for-mah)* .... form, shape
formulário, o *(for-moo-lah-ree-oo)* .... form
fortuna, a *(for-too-nah)* .... fortune
fotografia, a *(foh-toh-grah-fee-ah)* .... photograph
França, a *(frahn-sah)* .... France
francês *(frahn-saysh)* .... French
frango, o *(frahn-goo)* .... chicken
frase, a *(frah-zee)* .... sentence, phrase
freqüência, a *(freh-kwane-see-ah)* .... frequency
freqüente *(freh-kwehn-chee)* .... frequent
frio *(free-oo)* .... cold
frito/a *(free-too)* .... fried
fruta, a *(froo-tah)* .... fruit
frutos do mar, os *(froo-toosh)(doh)(mar)* ..... seafood
futebol, o *(foo-cheh-bohl)* .... soccer, football
futuro, o *(foo-too-roo)* .... future

G

galáxia, a *(gah-lahk-see-ah)* .... galaxy
galeria, a *(gah-leh-ree-ah)* .... gallery
garagem, a *(gah-rah-zhame)* .... garage
garçom, o *(gar-sohm)* .... waiter
garçonete, a *(gar-soh-neh-chee)* .... waitress
garfo, o *(gar-foo)* .... fork
garrafa, a *(gar-hah-fah)* .... bottle
gato, o *(gah-too)* .... cat
geladeira, a *(zheh-lah-day-rah)* .... refrigerator
geléia, a *(zheh-lay-ah)* .... jam, jelly
gelo, o *(zheh-loo)* .... ice
glória, a *(gloh-ree-ah)* .... glory
gorjeta, a *(gor-zheh-tah)* .... tip
gostaria de *(gohs-tah-ree-ah)(deh)* .... (I) would like

grande *(grahn-jee)* .... large, big
grande armazém, o *(grahn-jee)(ar-mah-zame)* . department store
gratinado/a *(grah-chee-nah-doo)* .... grated
graus, os *(grouse)* .... degrees
gravata, a *(grah-vah-tah)* .... tie
grave *(grah-vee)* .... grave, serious
grelhado/a *(grehl-yah-doo)* .... grilled
grupo, o *(groo-poo)* .... group
guarda-chuva, o *(gwahr-dah-shoo-vah)* .... umbrella
guardanapo, o *(gwahr-dah-nah-poo)* .... napkin

H

há *(ah)* .... there is, there are
habitual *(ah-bee-too-ahl)* .... habitual
história, a *(ees-toh-ree-ah)* .... history
hoje *(oh-zhee)* .... today
homem, o *(oh-mehn)* .... man
Honduras, a *(ohn-doo-rahs)* .... Honduras
honesto *(oh-nehs-too)* .... honest
honra, a *(ohn-hah)* .... honor
hora, a *(oh-rah)* .... hour, time
horário, o *(oh-rah-ree-oo)* .... timetable
hotel, o *(oh-tel)* .... hotel
humor, o *(oo-mor)* .... humor

I

idéia, a *(ee-day-ah)* .... idea
igreja, a *(ee-greh-zhah)* .... church
ilegal *(ee-leh-gahl)* .... illegal
iluminação, a *(ee-loo-mee-nah-sown)* .... lights
imaginação, a *(ee-mah-zhee-nah-sown)* .... imagination
importância, a *(eem-por-tahn-see-ah)* .... importance
importante *(eem-por-tahn-chee)* .... important
impossível *(eem-pohs-see-vel)* .... impossible
incêndio, o *(een-sane-jee-oo)* .... fire
incluído/a *(een-kloo-ee-doo)* .... included
incorreto/a *(een-kor-heh-too)* .... incorrect
influência, a *(een-floo-ayn-see-ah)* .... influence
informação, a *(een-for-mah-sown)* .... information
Inglaterra, a *(een-glah-tair-hah)* .... England
inglês *(een-glaysh)* .... English
ingresso, o *(een-grehs-soo)* .... ticket
instrução, a *(een-stroo-sown)* .... instruction
instrumento, o *(een-stroo-mehn-too)* .... instrument
inteligência, a *(een-teh-lee-zhayn-see-ah)* ...... intelligence
intenção, a *(een-tehn-sown)* .... intention
interessante *(een-teh-rehs-sahn-chee)* .... interesting
interior, o *(een-teh-ree-or)* .... interior
internacional *(een-tair-nah-see-oh-nahl)* ..... international
inverno, o *(een-vair-noo)* .... winter
ir *(eer)* .... to go
ir de avião *(eer)(jee)(ah-vee-own)* ...... to go by plane, to fly
ir de carro *(eer)(jee)(kar-hoo)* .... to go by car, to drive
Irlanda do Norte, a *(eer-lahn-dah)(doo)(nor-chee)* ....
.... Northern Ireland
irmã, a *(eer-mahn)* .... sister
irmão, o *(eer-mown)* .... brother
isso *(ees-soo)* .... that
Itália, a *(ee-tah-lee-ah)* .... Italy

J

janeiro *(zhah-nay-roo)* .... January
janela, a *(zhah-neh-lah)* .... window
jantar, o *(zhahn-tar)* .... dinner
japonês *(zhah-poh-naysh)* .... Japanese
jaqueta, a *(zhah-kay-tah)* .... jacket
jardim, o *(zhar-deem)* .... garden
jardim botânico, o *(zhar-deem)(boh-tah-nee-koo)* ....
.... botanical garden
jardim zoológico, o *(zhar-deem)(zoh-oh-loh-zhee-koo)* ... zoo
jeans, os *(jeansh)* .... jeans
jogo, o *(zhoh-goo)* .... game
jóias, as *(zhoy-ahs)* .... gemstones
jornal, o *(zhor-nahl)* .... newspaper

jornaleiro, o *(zhor-nah-lay-roo)* .... newsstand
jornalista, a/o *(zhor-nah-lees-tah)* .... journalist
jovem *(zhoh-vame)* .... young
judeu *(zhoo-deh-oo)* .... Jewish (♂)
judia *(zhoo-jee-ah)* .... Jewish (♀)
julho *(zhool-yoo)* .... July
junho *(zhoon-yoo)* .... June
justiça, a *(zhoos-chee-sah)* .... justice

L

lanchonete, a *(lahn-shoh-neh-chee)* .... informal restaurant
lápis, o *(lah-peesh)* .... pencil
laranja *(lah-rahn-zhah)* .... orange (color)
laranja, a *(lah-rahn-zhah)* .... orange (fruit)
lavanderia, a *(lah-vahn-deh-ree-ah)* .... laundry
lavar *(lah-var)* .... to wash
Leblon *(leh-blohn)* .... area of Rio
legal *(leh-gahl)* .... legal, cool
legume, o *(leh-goo-mee)* .... vegetable
leia *(lay-ah)* .... read!
leite, o *(lay-chee)* .... milk
lembrança, a *(lame-brahn-sah)* .... souvenir
lenço, o *(lehn-soo)* .... handkerchief
ler *(lair)* .... to read
leste *(lehs-chee)* .... east
lição, a *(lee-sown)* .... lesson
licor, o *(lee-kor)* .... liquor
limão, o *(lee-mown)* .... lime
limonada, a *(lee-moh-nah-dah)* .... lemonade
limpo/a *(leem-poo)* .... clean
linha, a *(leen-yah)* .... line
lista, a *(lees-tah)* .... list
lista telefônica, a *(lees-tah)(teh-leh-foh-nee-kah)* ....
.... telephone book
litro, o *(lee-troo)* .... liter
livraria, a *(lee-vrah-ree-ah)* .... bookstore
livre *(lee-vree)* .... free, available
livro, o *(lee-vroo)* .... book
local *(loh-kahl)* .... local
loja, a *(loh-zhah)* .... store
loja de material fotográfico, a *(loh-zhah)(jeh)(mah-teh-ree-ahl)(foh-toh-grah-fee-koo)* .... camera store
longo/a *(lohn-goo)* .... long
luvas, as *(loo-vahs)* .... gloves

M

maçã, a *(mah-sah)* .... apple
mãe, a *(mah-een)* .... mother
magazine, o *(mah-gah-zee-nee)* ... department store (Brazil)
maio *(my-oo)* .... May
maiô, o *(my-oh)* .... swimsuit (♂)
mais *(mysh)* .... more
mal *(mahl)* .... badly
mala, a *(mah-lah)* .... suitcase
mandar *(mahn-dar)* .... to send
manhã, a *(mahn-yahn)* .... morning
manteiga, a *(mahn-tay-gah)* .... butter
mapa, o *(mah-pah)* .... map
máquina, a *(mah-kee-nah)* .... machine
máquina fotográfica, a *(mah-kee-nah)(foh-toh-grah-fee-kah)* .... camera
maracujá, a *(mah-rah-koo-zhah)* .... passion fruit
março *(mar-soo)* .... March
marrom *(mar-hohm)* .... brown
masculino *(mahs-koo-lee-noo)* .... masculine
matemática, a *(mah-teh-mah-chee-kah)* ...... mathematics
matrimônio, o *(mah-tree-moh-nee-oo)* ..... matrimony
mau *(mow)* .... bad
máximo/a *(mah-see-moo)* .... maximum
me dá *(mee)(dah)* .... give me!
mecânico, o *(meh-kah-nee-koo)* .... mechanic
medicina, a *(meh-jee-see-nah)* .... medicine
médico, o *(meh-jee-koo)* .... doctor
mediterrâneo, o *(meh-jee-tair-hah-neh-oo)* .. Mediterranean

meia, a *(may-ah)* .... sock
meia *(may-ah)* .... six (when saying telephone numbers)
meia-calça, a *(may-ah-kahl-sah)* .... pantyhose
meia-dúzia, a *(may-ah-doo-zee-ah)* .... half-dozen
meia-noite, a *(may-ah-noy-chee)* .... midnight
meio/a *(may-oo)* .... half
meio-dia, o *(may-oo-jee-ah)* .... noon
melodia, a *(meh-loh-jee-ah)* .... melody
menina, a *(meh-nee-nah)* .... girl
menino, o *(meh-nee-noo)* .... boy
mensagem de texto, a *(men-sah-zhame)(jeh)(tesh-too)* . text message
menu, o *(meh-noo)* .... menu
mercado, o *(mair-kah-doo)* .... market
mês, o *(maysh)* .... month
mesa, a *(meh-zah)* .... table, desk
metro, o *(meh-troo)* .... meter
metrô, o *(meh-troh)* .... metro, subway
metropolitano/a *(meh-troh-poh-lee-tah-noo)* .. metropolitan
meu *(meh-oo)* .... my
México, o *(meh-shee-koo)* .... Mexico
mil *(meel)* .... thousand
mínimo/a *(mee-nee-moo)* .... minimum
ministro, o *(mee-nees-troo)* .... minister (government)
minuto, o *(mee-noo-too)* .... minute
misto/a *(mees-too)* .... mixed
Moçambique, o *(moh-sahm-bee-kee)* .... Mozambique
moderno/a *(moh-dair-noo)* .... modern
modo, o *(moh-doo)* .... means, way
moeda, a *(moh-eh-dah)* .... coin
momento, o *(moh-mehn-too)* .... moment
monastério, o *(moh-nahs-teh-ree-oo)* ...... monastery
montanha, a *(mohn-tahn-yah)* .... mountain
morango, o *(moh-rahn-goo)* .... strawberry
motocicleta, a *(moh-toh-see-kleh-tah)* .... motorcycle
mousse, a *(mohs-see)* .... mousse
móveis, os *(moh-vaysh)* .... furniture
muito/a *(mwee-too)* .... very, a lot
mulher, a *(mool-yair)* .... woman
multicolorido/a *(mool-chee-koh-loh-ree-doo)* .. multi-colored
municipal *(moo-nee-see-pahl)* .... municipal
museu, o *(moo-zeh-oo)* .... museum
música, a *(moo-zee-kah)* .... music
musical *(moo-zee-kahl)* .... musical

N

na (em + a) *(nah)* .... in the, into the
nada *(nah-dah)* .... nothing
não *(nown)* .... no
não ... nada *(nown)* ... *(nah-dah)* .... nothing
não é? *(nown)(eh)* .... isn't it?
não gosto *(nown)(gohs-too)* ...... (I) do not like it
Natal, o *(nah-tahl)* .... Christmas
natural *(nah-too-rahl)* .... natural
naturalmente *(nah-too-rahl-mehn-chee)* .... naturally
náutico/a *(now-chee-koo)* .... nautical
necessário/a *(neh-sehs-sah-ree-oo)* .... necessary
neva *(neh-vah)* .... it snows
névoa, a *(neh-voh-ah)* .... fog
no (em + o) *(noh)* .... in, in the, into the
noite, a *(noy-chee)* .... evening, night
nome, o *(noh-mee)* .... name
normal *(nor-mahl)* .... normal
norte *(nor-chee)* .... north
nós *(noys)* .... we
nos *(nohs)* .... in the
nota, a *(noh-tah)* .... bill (currency)
nove *(noh-vee)* .... nine
novembro *(noh-vem-broo)* .... November
noventa *(noh-vehn-tah)* .... ninety
novo/a *(noh-voo)* .... new
número, o *(noo-meh-roo)* .... number

O

o *(oh)* .... the
o que *(oh)(kay)* .... what

objeto, o *(ohb-zheh-too)* .... object
obrigada *(oh-bree-gah-dah)* .... thank you (♠)
obrigado *(oh-bree-gah-doo)* .... thank you (♦)
ocasião, a *(oh-kah-zee-own)* .... occasion
oceano, o *(oh-seh-ah-noo)* .... ocean
ocidente, o *(oh-see-dehn-chee)* .... occident, west
óculos, os *(oh-koo-loosh)* .... eyeglasses
óculos de sol, os *(oh-koo-loosh)(jee)(sohl)* ...... sunglasses
ocupado/a *(oh-koo-pah-doo)* .... occupied, busy
oeste *(oh-ehs-chee)* .... west
oi *(oy)* .... hi, hello
oitenta *(oy-tehn-tah)* .... eighty
oito *(oy-too)* .... eight
olá *(oh-lah)* .... hi, hello
onde *(ohn-jee)* .... where
ônibus, o *(ow-nee-boos)* .... bus
ontem *(ohn-tame)* .... yesterday
onze *(ohn-zee)* .... eleven
opção, a *(ohp-sown)* .... option
ópera, a *(oh-peh-rah)* .... opera
operação, a *(oh-peh-rah-sown)* .... operation
oportunidade, a *(oh-por-too-nee-dah-jee)* ... opportunity
oposição, a *(oh-poh-zee-sown)* .... opposition
ordinário/a *(or-jee-nah-ree-oo)* .... ordinary
orelhão, o *(oh-rel-yown)* .... nickname for telephone booth
oriental *(oh-ree-ehn-tahl)* .... oriental
original *(oh-ree-zhee-nahl)* .... original
os *(ohs)* .... the (plural)
ostra, a *(ohs-trah)* .... oyster
ou *(oh)* .... or
outono, o *(oh-toh-noo)* .... autumn
outubro *(oh-too-broo)* .... October
oval *(oh-vahl)* .... oval
ovo, o *(oh-voo)* .... egg

P

pacote, o *(pah-koh-chee)* .... package
padaria, a *(pah-dah-ree-ah)* .... bakery
pagar *(pah-gar)* .... to pay, to pay for
página, a *(pah-zhee-nah)* .... page
pai, o *(pie)* .... father
pais, os *(piesh)* .... parents
palácio, o *(pah-lah-see-oo)* .... palace
palavra, a *(pah-lah-vrah)* .... word
palavras cruzadas, as *(pah-lah-vrahs)(kroo-zah-dahs)* .....
.... crossword puzzle
palma, a *(pahl-mah)* .... palm
Panamá, o *(pah-nah-mah)* .... Panama
pânico, o *(pah-nee-koo)* .... panic
pão, o *(pown)* .... bread
Pão de Açúcar, o *(pown)(jeh)(ah-soo-kar)* .Sugar Loaf (in Rio)
papel, o *(pah-pel)* .... paper
papelaria, a *(pah-peh-lah-ree-ah)* ..... stationery store
para *(pah-rah)* .... to, for
parada, a *(pah-rah-dah)* .... stop
Paraguai, o *(pah-rah-gwhy)* .... Paraguay
pare *(pah-ree)* .... stop!
parentes, os *(pah-rehn-cheesh)* .... relatives
partida, a *(par-chee-dah)* .... departure
partir *(par-cheer)* .... to depart
Páscoa, a *(pahs-koh-ah)* .... Easter
passagem, a *(pahs-sah-zhame)* .... ticket
passaporte, o *(pahs-sah-por-chee)* .... passport
pasta de dentes, a *(pahs-tah)(jeh)(dehn-chees)* .. toothpaste
pausa, a *(pow-zah)* .... pause
pedir *(peh-jeer)* .... to order, to request
peixaria, a *(pay-shah-ree-ah)* .... fish store
peixe, o *(pay-shee)* .... fish
pente, o *(pehn-chee)* .... comb
pequeno almoço, o *(peh-kay-noo)(ahl-moh-soo)* .. breakfast
pequeno/a *(peh-kay-noo)* .... small
pêra, a *(pair-ah)* .... pear
perder *(pair-dair)* .... to lose
perfeito/a *(pair-fay-too)* .... perfect

perfume, o *(pair-foo-mee)* .... perfume
pergunta, a *(pair-goon-tah)* .... question
perguntar *(pair-goon-tar)* .... to question
Peru, o *(peh-roo)* .... Peru
perucas, as *(peh-roo-kahs)* .... wigs
pia, a *(pee-ah)* .... washstand, sink
pianista, o/a *(pee-ah-nees-tah)* .... pianist
piano, o *(pee-ah-noo)* .... piano
pijama, o *(pee-zhah-mah)* .... pajamas
piloto, o *(pee-loh-too)* .... pilot
pimenta, a *(pee-mehn-tah)* .... pepper
piso, o *(pee-zoo)* .... floor
planetário, o *(plah-neh-tah-ree-oo)* .... planetarium
plataforma, a *(plah-tah-for-mah)* .... platform
pobre *(poh-bree)* .... poor
pode *(poh-jee)* .... (you) can
poder *(poh-dair)* .... to be able to, can
pois não *(poysh)(nown)* .... of course
polícia, a *(poh-lee-see-ah)* .... police
política, a *(poh-lee-chee-kah)* .... politics
Pólo Norte, o *(poh-loo)(nor-chee)* .... North Pole
Pólo Sul, o *(poh-loo)(sool)* .... South Pole
ponto, o *(pohn-too)* .... point
ponto de ônibus, o *(pohn-too)(jee)(ow-nee-boos)* ... bus stop
ponto de táxi, o *(pohn-too)(jee)(tahk-see)* .... taxi stand
ponto de vista, o *(pohn-too)(jeh)(vees-tah)* .... viewpoint
por favor *(por)(fah-vor)* . please, excuse me (to catch attention)
por que *(por)(kay)* .... why
porão, o *(poh-rown)* .... basement
porcelana, a *(por-seh-lah-nah)* .... porcelain
porco, o *(por-koo)* .... pork
porta, a *(por-tah)* .... door
portão, o *(por-town)* .... gate
porto, o *(por-too)* .... port wine
Portugal, o *(por-too-gahl)* .... Portugal
português *(por-too-gaysh)* .... Portuguese
possível *(pohs-see-vel)* .... possible
posso *(pohs-soo)* .... (I) can
posto de gasolina, o *(pohs-too)(jee)(gah-zoh-lee-nah)* ...
.... service station, gas station
pouco/a *(poh-koo)* .... a little
pousada, a *(poh-zah-dah)* ..... small hotel, inn
praia, a *(pry-ah)* .... beach
prática, a *(prah-chee-kah)* .... practice
prato, o *(prah-too)* .... plate
prato feito, o *(prah-too)(fay-too)* ... reasonably priced meal
precioso/a *(preh-see-oh-zoo)* .... precious
precisar de *(preh-see-zar)(dee)* .... to need, to have need of
preciso/a *(preh-see-zoo)* .... precise
preço, o *(preh-soo)* .... price
preparo, o *(preh-pah-roo)* .... preparation
presente, o *(preh-zehn-chee)* .... present, gift
presunto, o *(preh-zoon-too)* .... ham
preto *(preh-too)* .... black
primavera, a *(pree-mah-veh-rah)* .... spring
primeiro/a *(pree-may-roo)* .... first
principal *(preen-see-pahl)* .... principal, main
problema, o *(proh-bleh-mah)* .... problem
produto, o *(proh-doo-too)* .... product
professor, o *(proh-fehs-sor)* .... professor
programa, o *(proh-grah-mah)* .... program
proibido/a *(proh-ee-bee-doo)* .... prohibited
promessa, a *(proh-mehs-sah)* .... promise
pronúncia, a *(proh-noon-see-ah)* .... pronunciation
protestante *(proh-tehs-tahn-chee)* .... Protestant
público, o *(poo-blee-koo)* .... public
purê de batatas, o *(poo-ray)(jee)(bah-tah-tahs)* ....
.... mashed potatoes
púrpura *(poor-poo-rah)* .... purple
puxe *(poo-shee)* .... pull! (doors)

Q

quadro, o *(kwah-droo)* .... picture
qual *(kwahl)* .... which, what

quando *(kwahn-doo)* .... when
quanto *(kwahn-too)* .... how much
Quanto custa isso? *(kwahn-too)(koos-tah)(ees-soo)* ....
.... How much does that cost?
quantos/quantas *(kwahn-toosh)/(kwahn-tahs)* ... how many
quarenta *(kwah-rehn-tah)* .... forty
quarta-feira, a *(kwahr-tah-fay-rah)* .... Wednesday
quarto, o *(kwahr-too)* .... bedroom
quatorze *(kwah-tor-zee)* .... fourteen
quatro *(kwah-troo)* .... four
que *(kay)* .... what
Que horas são? *(kay)(oh-rahs)(sown)* ..... What time is it?
queijo, o *(kay-zhoo)* .... cheese
quem *(kame)* .... who
quente *(kane-chee)* .... hot
querer *(kair-air)* .... to want
quero *(kair-oo)* .... (I) want
quinhentos *(keen-yehn-toosh)* .... five hundred
quinta-feira, a *(keen-tah-fay-rah)* .... Thursday
quinze *(keen-zee)* .... fifteen, quarter (time)

R

R$ .... abbreviation for **real** (Brazilian currency)
raça, a *(hah-sah)* .... race
rádio, o *(hah-joo)* .... radio
raio, o *(hi-oo)* .... ray
rápido/a *(hah-pee-doo)* .... rapid
reação, a *(heh-ah-sown)* .... reaction
reais, os *(heh-eyes)* .... reals
real, o *(heh-ahl)* .... real (unit of Brazilian currency)
rebelião, a *(heh-beh-lee-own)* .... rebellion
receber *(heh-seh-bair)* .... to receive
recebimento de bagagem, o *(heh-seh-bee-mehn-too)(jee)*
(bah-gah-zhame) .... baggage claim
refeição, a *(heh-fay-sown)* .... meal
refrigerante, o *(heh-free-zheh-rahn-chee)* ...... soft drink
regular *(heh-goo-lar)* .... regular
relação, a *(heh-lah-sown)* .... relation
relaxado/a *(heh-lah-shah-doo)* .... relaxed
religião, a *(heh-lee-zhee-own)* .... religion
relógio, o *(heh-loh-zhee-oo)* .... clock, watch
relojoaria, a *(heh-loh-zhoh-ah-ree-ah)* ... watchmaker's shop
repetir *(heh-peh-cheer)* .... to repeat
repita por favor *(heh-pee-tah)(por)(fah-vor)* .. please repeat!
república, a *(heh-poo-blee-kah)* .... republic
reserva, a *(heh-zair-vah)* .... reservation
reservar *(heh-zair-var)* .... to reserve
resposta, a *(hehs-pohs-tah)* .... answer
restaurante, o *(hehs-tow-rahn-chee)* .... restaurant
revista, a *(heh-vees-tah)* .... magazine
revolução, a *(heh-voh-loo-sown)* .... revolution
rico/a *(hee-koo)* .... rich
rodoviária, a *(hoh-doh-vee-ah-ree-ah)* ... bus station
romano/a *(hoh-mah-noo)* .... Roman
romântico/a *(hoh-mahn-chee-koo)* .... romantic
rosa *(hoh-zah)* .... pink
roupa, a *(hoh-pah)* .... clothing
roupa de cama, a *(hoh-pah)(jee)(kah-mah)* ...... bedding
roupão de banho, o *(hoh-pown)(jeh)(bahn-yoo)* ... bathrobe
roupas íntimas, as *(hoh-pahs)(een-chee-mahs)* .... lingerie
rua, a *(hoo-ah)* .... street
rubi, o *(hoo-bee)* .... ruby
russo *(hoos-soo)* .... Russian

S

sábado, o *(sah-bah-doo)* .... Saturday
saber *(sah-bair)* .... to know (a fact), to know (how to)
sabonete, o *(sah-boh-neh-chee)* .... soap
saia, a *(sy-ah)* .... skirt
saída de emergência, a *(sah-ee-dah)(jeh)(eh-mair-zhayn-see-ah)* .... emergency exit
saída, a *(sah-ee-dah)* .... exit
sal, o *(sahl)* .... salt
sala de espera, a *(sah-lah)(jeh)(es-peh-rah)* ... waiting room

sala de jantar, a *(sah-lah)(deh)(zhahn-tar)* ..... dining room
sala, a *(sah-lah)* .... living room
salada, a *(sah-lah-dah)* .... salad
salário, o *(sah-lah-ree-oo)* .... salary
salmão, o *(sahl-mown)* .... salmon
sandálias, as *(sahn-dah-lee-ahs)* .... sandals
sanduíche, o *(sahn-doo-ee-shee)* .... sandwich
santo, o *(sahn-too)* .... saint
são *(sown)* .... are
sapatos, os *(sah-pah-toosh)* .... shoes
sardinha, a *(sar-jeen-yah)* .... sardine
saudável *(sow-dah-vel)* .... healthy
se diz *(seh)(jeesh)* .... one says
seção de não fumantes, a *(seh-sown)(jee)(nown)(foo-mahn-*
chees) .... non-smoking section
seção de perdidos e achados, a *(seh-sown)(jeh)(pair-jee-*
doosh)(eh)(ah-shah-doosh) ... lost-and-found office
secretária, a *(seh-kreh-tah-ree-ah)* .... secretary (♀)
secretário, o *(seh-kreh-tah-ree-oo)* .... secretary (♂)
sede, a *(seh-jee)* .... thirst
seguinte *(seh-geen-chee)* .... following
segunda *(seh-goon-dah)* .... second
segunda-feira, a *(seh-goon-dah-fay-rah)* .... Monday
segundo, o *(seh-goon-doo)* .... second (time)
seis *(saysh)* .... six
seleção, a *(seh-leh-sown)* .... selection
selo, o *(seh-loo)* .... stamp
sem *(same)* .... without
semana, a *(seh-mah-nah)* .... week
senhor, o *(sehn-yor)* .... Mr., sir
senhora, a *(sehn-yoh-rah)* .... Mrs., Ms.
senhorita, a *(sehn-yoh-ree-tah)* .... Miss
sensação, a *(sehn-sah-sown)* .... sensation
sentado *(sehn-tah-doo)* .... seated
serviço, o *(sair-vee-soo)* .... service
serviços ao cliente, os *(sair-vee-soosh)(ah-oh)(klee-ehn-chee)* .... customer service
servir *(sair-veer)* .... to fit (clothing), to serve
sessenta *(sehs-sehn-tah)* .... sixty
sete *(seh-chee)* .... seven
setembro *(seh-tem-broo)* .... September
setenta *(seh-tehn-tah)* .... seventy
seu *(seh-oo)* .... your, his, her, its
severo/a *(seh-veh-roo)* .... severe
sexta-feira, a *(saysh-tah-fay-rah)* .... Friday
short, o *(shorch)* .... shorts
sidra, a *(see-drah)* .... cider
siga *(see-gah)* .... continue!
silêncio, o *(see-lane-see-oo)* .... silence
sim *(seem)* .... yes
simples *(seem-pleesh)* .... simple
simultâneo/a *(see-mool-tah-neh-oo)* .... simultaneous
sinfonia, a *(seen-foh-nee-ah)* .... symphony
sistema, o *(sees-teh-mah)* .... system
sobre *(soh-bree)* .... on top of, over, on
sobremesa, a *(soh-breh-meh-zah)* .... dessert
social *(soh-see-ahl)* .... social
sofá, o *(soh-fah)* .... sofa
sólido/a *(soh-lee-doo)* .... solid
sopa, a *(soh-pah)* .... soup
sorvete, o *(sor-veh-chee)* .... ice cream
sou *(soh)* .... (I) am
sua *(soo-ah)* .... your
suco, o *(soo-koo)* .... juice
suéter, a *(soo-eh-tair)* .... sweater
Suíça, a *(swee-sah)* .... Switzerland
sul *(sool)* .... south
sunga, a *(soon-gah)* .... swimsuit (♂)
supermercado, o *(soo-pair-mair-kah-doo)* ... supermarket
sutiã, o *(soo-chee-own)* .... bra

T

tabaco, o *(tah-bah-koo)* .... tobacco
talho, o *(tahl-yoo)* .... butcher shop (Portugal)
tamanho, o *(tah-mahn-yoo)* .... size

também *(tahm-bame)* .... also
tapete, o *(tah-peh-chee)* .... carpet
tarde, a *(tar-jee)* .... afternoon
tarifa, a *(tah-ree-fah)* .... tariff, fare
táxi, o *(tahk-see)* .... taxi
tchau *(chow)* .... good-bye, bye
teatro, o *(teh-ah-troo)* .... theater
técnico/a *(tek-nee-koo)* .... technical
telefonar *(teh-leh-foh-nar)* .... to telephone, to call
telefone, o *(teh-leh-foh-nee)* .... telephone
telefone celular, o *(teh-leh-foh-nee)(sel-oo-lar)* .. cell phone
telefonista, a *(teh-leh-foh-nees-tah)* .... operator
telegrama, o *(teh-leh-grah-mah)* .... telegram
televisão, a *(teh-leh-vee-zown)* .... television
tem *(tame)* .... (you) have
temperatura, a *(tame-peh-rah-too-rah)* ... temperature
tempo, o *(tame-poo)* .... weather
tenho *(tehn-yoo)* .... (I) have
tênis, os *(tay-nees)* .... tennis shoes
ter *(tair)* .... to have
ter que *(tair)(kay)* .... to have to, must
terça-feira, a *(tair-sah-fay-rah)* .... Tuesday
terçeiro/a *(tair-say-roo)* .... third
terminal, o *(tair-mee-nahl)* .... terminal
termômetro, o *(tair-moh-meh-troo)* ... thermometer
terno, o *(tair-noo)* .... suit
térreo, o *(tair-heh-oo)* .... ground floor
tia, a *(chee-ah)* .... aunt
tinturaria, a *(cheen-too-rah-ree-ah)* ..... dry cleaners
tio, o *(chee-oo)* .... uncle
típico/a *(chee-pee-koo)* .... typical
tira-gosto, o *(chee-rah-gohs-too)* .... appetizer
toalha, a *(toh-ahl-yah)* .... towel
tomar *(toh-mar)* .... to take
tomate, o *(toh-mah-chee)* .... tomato
torta, a *(tor-tah)* .... pie
total, o *(toh-tahl)* .... total
tráfego, o *(trah-feh-goo)* .... traffic
trágico/a *(trah-zhee-koo)* .... tragic
tranqüilo/a *(trahn-kwee-loo)* .... tranquil, quiet
transparente *(trahns-pah-rehn-chee)* .... transparent
transportar *(trahns-por-tar)* .... to transport
travesseiro, o *(trah-vehs-say-roo)* .... pillow
trem, o *(trame)* .... train
três *(traysh)* .... three
treze *(treh-zee)* .... thirteen
trezentos *(treh-zehn-toosh)* .... three hundred
triângulo, o *(tree-ahn-goo-loo)* .... triangle
tribunal de justiça, o *(tree-boo-nahl)(deh)(zhoos-chee-sah)* ..
.... courthouse, Court of Justice
trinta *(treen-tah)* .... thirty
triunfante *(tree-oon-fahn-chee)* .... triumphant
trivial *(tree-vee-ahl)* .... trivial
trocar *(troh-kar)*... to transfer (vehicles), to change (money)
troco, o *(troh-koo)* .... change (money)
trompeta, a *(trohm-peh-tah)* .... trumpet
tropical *(troh-pee-kahl)* .... tropical
tu *(too)* .... you (familiar)
tudo *(too-doo)* .... everything
Tudo bem? *(too-doo)(bame)* .... How's it going?
tumulto, o *(too-mool-too)* .... tumult
túnel, o *(too-nel)* .... tunnel
turismo, o *(too-rees-moo)* .... tourism
turista, o/a *(too-rees-tah)* .... tourist
tutor, o *(too-tor)* .... tutor

U

último/a *(ool-chee-moo)* .... ultimate, last
ultrapassar *(ool-trah-pahs-sar)* .... to pass (vehicles)
um *(oom)* .... a, an (♂, singular)
uma *(oo-mah)* .... a, an (♀, singular)
união, a *(oo-nee-own)* .... union
uniforme, o *(oo-nee-for-mee)* .... uniform
universidade, a *(oo-nee-vair-see-dah-jee)* .... university
urgência, a *(oor-zhayn-see-ah)* .... urgency

urgente *(oor-zhehn-chee)* .... urgent
Uruguai, o *(oo-roo-gwhy)* .... Uruguay
usado/a *(oo-zah-doo)* .... used
usar *(oo-zar)* .... to use
usual *(oo-zoo-ahl)* .... usual
utensílio, o *(oo-tehn-see-lee-oo)* .... utensil
utilidade, a *(oo-chee-lee-dah-jee)* .... utility

V

vaca, a *(vah-kah)* .... beef
vacina, a *(vah-see-nah)* .... vaccine
vaga, a *(vah-gah)* .... vacancy
vagão, o *(vah-gown)* .... wagon, compartment
vai *(vy)* .... go!
vaidade, a *(vy-dah-jee)* .... vanity
vale, o *(vah-lee)* .... valley
válido/a *(vah-lee-doo)* .... valid
variedade, a *(vah-ree-eh-dah-jee)* .... variety
vários/as *(vah-ree-oosh)* .... various
vaso sanitário, o *(vah-zoo)(sah-nee-tah-ree-oo)* ..... toilet
vaso, o *(vah-zoo)* .... vase
Vaticano, o *(vah-chee-kah-noo)* .... the Vatican
vegetariano, o *(veh-zheh-tah-ree-ah-noo)* .... vegetarian
veículo, o *(veh-ee-koo-loo)* .... vehicle
velho/a *(vel-yoo)* .... old
velocidade, a *(veh-loh-see-dah-jee)* .... velocity, speed
vem *(vame)* .... comes
vender *(vehn-dair)* .... to sell
Venezuela, a *(veh-neh-zoo-eh-lah)* .... Venezuela
venta *(vehn-tah)* .... it is windy
ver *(vair)* .... to see
verão, o *(veh-rown)* .... summer
verbo, o *(vair-boo)* .... verb
vermelho/a *(vair-mel-yoo)* ....red
véspera de ano novo, a *(vehs-peh-rah)(jee)(ah-noo)(noh-voo)*
.... New Year's Eve
véspera de Natal, a *(vehs-peh-rah)(jeh)(nah-tahl)*..........
.... Christmas Eve
vestido, o *(vehs-chee-doo)* .... dress
vestir *(vehs-cheer)* .... to fit (clothing), to wear
vestuário, o *(vehs-too-ah-ree-oo)* .... clothing
via aérea *(vee-ah)(ah-air-ee-ah)* .... by airmail
viagem, a *(vee-ah-zhame)* .... trip
viajante, o/a *(vee-ah-zhahn-chee)* .... traveler
viajar *(vee-ah-zhar)* .... to travel
vídeos, os *(vee-joosh)* .... videos
vinagre, o *(vee-nah-gree)* .... vinegar
vinho, o *(veen-yoo)* .... wine
vinho tinto, o *(veen-yoo)(cheen-too)* .... red wine
vinte *(veen-chee)* .... twenty
violeta *(vee-oh-leh-tah)* .... violet
violino, o *(vee-oh-lee-noo)* .... violin
vir *(veer)* .... to come
virar *(vee-rar)* .... to turn
vire *(vee-ree)* .... turn!
visa, a *(vee-zah)* .... visa
viseira, a *(vee-zay-rah)* .... visor
visita, a *(vee-zee-tah)* .... visit
visitar *(vee-zee-tar)* .... to visit
vista, a *(vees-tah)* .... view
vitamina, a *(vee-tah-mee-nah)* ..... milk blended with fruit
vitela, a *(vee-teh-lah)* .... veal
viver *(vee-vair)* .... to live
você *(voh-say)* .... you
vocês *(voh-saysh)* .... you (plural)

X

xícara, a *(shee-kah-rah)* .... cup

Z

zero *(zeh-roo)* .... zero
zodíaco, o *(zoh-jee-ah-koo)* .... zodiac
zona, a *(zoh-nah)* .... zone
zoologia, a *(zoh-oh-loh-zhee-ah)* .... zoology

This beverage guide is intended to explain the variety of beverages available to you while **em Brasil ou** any other Portuguese-speaking country. It is by no means complete. Some of the experimenting has been left up to you, but this should get you started.

BEBIDAS QUENTES (hot drinks)

café / cafezinho . . . . coffee
café com leite . . . . coffee with milk
espresso . . . . espresso
capuccino . . . . capuccino
chocolate quente . . . . hot chocolate

chá . . . . tea
chá com limão . . . . tea with lemon
chá com leite . . . . tea with milk

BEBIDAS FRIAS (cold drinks)

leite . . . . milk
milk-shake . . . . milkshake
vitamina . . . . milk and fruit drink
suco . . . . juice
  suco de laranja . . . . . orange juice
  suco de tomate . . . . . tomato juice
água . . . . water
água mineral . . . . mineral water
água com gás . . . . sparkling water
água tônica . . . . tonic water
sidra . . . . cider
chá mate . . . . Brazilian iced tea
refrigerante . . . . soft drink
guaraná . . . . soft drink made from
                       Amazonian berries
gelo . . . . ice

VINHOS (wine)

There are four main types of **vinho**, but quality levels vary drastically. **Vinho** can be purchased by the **garrafa** (bottle) or by the **copo** (glass).

vinho tinto . . . . red wine
vinho branco . . . . white wine
vinho rosé . . . . rosé wine
vinho tinto suave . . . light red wine

vinho de mesa . . . . . . ordinary table wine
vinho doce . . . . sweet wine
vinho seco . . . . dry wine
champanhe . . . . champagne
vinho do porto . . . . . . port wine
sangria . . . . wine drink made with
                       fruits, brandy, lemonade
                       and ice

CERVEJAS (beer)

There are many brands of beer. **Cerveja** is generally purchased by the **garrafa** (bottle) or **chope** (draught).

BEBIDAS ALCOÓLICAS (alcohol)

vodca . . . . vodka
uísque . . . . whiskey, bourbon
uísque escocês . . . scotch
gim . . . . gin
rum . . . . rum
cachaça . . . . liquor distilled directly from
                   the unrefined sugar cane,
                   fermented, then boiled down
                   to a concentrate; the national
                   drink of Brazil which retains
                   the scent of sugar cane
conhaque . . . . cognac
licor . . . . liqueur
batida . . . . cocktail of **cachaça** blended
                   with fruit and condensed
                   milk
caipirinha . . . . cocktail of **cachaça** lime
                   and sugar

O Cardápio
menu

Pão e Massa (bread and pasta)

pão	bread
bisnaga	baguette
pão integral	whole wheat bread
pão de milho	corn bread
pão de batata	potato bread
pão francês	French bread
torrada	toast
espagueti	spaghetti

Legumes (vegetables)

agrião	watercress
alcachofra	artichokes
alface	lettuce
aspargos	asparagus
batata doce	sweet potatoes
beringela	eggplant
beterrabas	beets
cebola	onions
cenoura	carrots
cogumelos	mushrooms
couve-flor	cauliflower
ervilhas	peas
espinafre	spinach
feijão	black beans
feijão roxo	kidney beans
lentilha	lentils
milho	corn
rabanete	radishes

Batatas (potatoes)

batatas assadas	baked potatoes
batatas cozidas	boiled potatoes
batatas fritas	French fried potatoes
batatas recheadas	stuffed potatoes
purê de batatas	mashed potatoes
salada de batatas	potato salad

Lingüiças (sausages)

salaminho	salami
lingüiça de porco	pork sausage
toucinho	bacon
presunto	ham

Fruta (fruit)

abacate	avocado
abacaxi	pineapple
ameixa	plum
banana	banana
cajú	cashew fruit
cereja	cherry
côco	coconut
coquetel de frutas	fruit cocktail
damasco	apricot
figo	fig
frambueza	raspberries
fruta-de conde	sweetsop
goiaba	guava
jaca	jackfruit
laranja	orange
limão	lime
maçã	apple
mamão	papaya
manga	mango
maracujá	passion fruit
melancia	watermelon
melão	melon
morango	strawberries
pêra	pear
pêssego	peach
uvas	grapes

Bebidas (beverages)

refrigerantes	soft drinks
cerveja	beer
leite	milk
café	coffee
suco de …	juice of …
limonada	lemonade
água mineral	mineral water

(bohm)   *(ah-peh-chee-chee)*

Bom apetite!
enjoy your meal

Modo de Preparo

à milanesa	in batter
ao forno	baked
assado	roasted
cozido	cooked, broiled
crú	raw
frito	fried
gratinado	grated, au gratin
grelhado	grilled
no vapor	steamed
picante	spicy
sauté	sautéed
mal passado	rare
ao ponto	medium
bem passado	well-done

Diversos (general)

alho	garlic
azeite	olive oil
geléia	jam
mel	honey
molho	sauce
mostarda	mustard
pimenta	pepper
queijo	cheese
sal	salt
vinagre	vinegar
bolo	cake
doce	pastry
sorvete	ice cream
creme chantilly	whipped cream

FOLD HERE

Tira-gostos (appetizers)

bolinho de bacalhau	codfish cake
bolinho de caranguejo	crab cake
coxinha de galinha	chicken croquettes
aipim frito	deep fried cassava
provolone à milanesa	breaded and fried provolone cheese balls
ostras	oysters
espeto de camarão	barbecued shrimp usually brought to you on the beach
caviar	caviar
porções variadas	assorted appetizers
frios	cold cuts
presunto defumado	smoked ham

Sopas (soups)

feijoada	stew of black beans, sausage, pork, dried beef, onions, garlic and tomato served with boiled rice and orange slices
canja de galinha	chicken soup
tutu	mush of beans, bacon, beef, sausage, manioc flour and onion
xinxim de galinha	spicy chicken and shrimp stew, served with rice

Ovos (eggs)

bem cozidos	hard-boiled eggs
mal cozidos	soft-boiled eggs
fritos	fried eggs
mexidos	scrambled eggs
poché	poached eggs
omelete de . . .	omelette with . . .
suflê	soufflé

Carne (meat)

churrasco	portions of barbecued meat

Vaca (beef)

almôndegas	meat balls
fígado	liver
filé	filet, steak
língua	tongue
rosbife	roast beef

Porco (pork)

costeleta de porco	pork chops
lombo	pork loin
lombo recheado	stuffed pork loin
porco assado	roast pork
presunto	ham

Cordeiro (lamb)

cordeiro assado	roast lamb
costeleta de cordeiro	lamb chops

Aves (poultry and game)

codorna	quail
coelho	rabbit
faisão	pheasant
frango	young chicken
galheto	grilled young chicken
galinha	chicken
pato	duck
pato ao tucupi	roast duck with a manioc juice
perdiz	partridge
peru	turkey

Sobremesas (desserts)

mousse de chocolate	chocolate mousse
mousse de maracujá	passion fruit mousse
pudim de leite	caramel flan
quindim	flan of egg yolk, coconut and sugar
Romeu e Julieta	guava paste and cheese with cream
sorvete de fruta	fruit ice cream
torta de morango	strawberry pie

Peixe e Frutos do Mar (fish and seafood)

acarajé	large fritter of black-eyed beans and shrimp
atum	tuna
bacalhau	cod
badejo	bass
camarão	prawns, shrimp
caranguejo	crab
lagosta	lobster
linguado	sole
lula	squid
mexilhão	mussels
moqueca	seafood stew
moqueca de camarão	shrimp stew
moqueca de peixe	halibut stew
siri	stuffed crab
sururu	mussel dish
truta	trout
vatapá	shrimp, coconut milk, nuts and spices served with rice
zarzuela de mariscos	thick seafood stew

Saladas (salads)

salada de alface	lettuce salad
salada de batata	potato salad
salada da casa	seasonal salad
salada de frutas	fruit salad
salada de legumes	vegetable salad
salada de mista	mixed salad
salada de pepino	cucumber salad
salada de tomate	tomato salad
salpicão de galinha	chicken salad

Acompanhamentos ou Guarnições (side dishes)

couve	collard greens
arroz	rice
farofa	manioc flour mixture
feijão	black beans
fubá	corn meal

Now that you've finished...

You've done it!

You've completed all the Steps, stuck your labels, flashed your cards, cut out your beverage and menu guides and practiced your new language. Do you realize how far you've come and how much you've learned? You've accomplished what it could take years to achieve in a traditional language class.

You can now confidently

- ask questions,
- understand directions,
- make reservations,
- order food and
- shop for anything.

And you can do it all in a foreign language! Go anywhere with confidence — from a large cosmopolitan restaurant to a small, out-of-the-way village where no one speaks English. Your experiences will be much more enjoyable and worry-free now that you speak the language.

As you've seen, learning a foreign language can be fun. Why limit yourself to just one? Now you're ready to learn another language with the *10 minutes a day*® Series!

Kris Kershul

Kristine Kershul

To place an order –

- Visit us at **www.bbks.com**, day or night.
- Call us at (800) 488-5068 or (206) 284-4211 between 8:00 a.m. and 5:00 p.m. Pacific Time, Monday - Friday.
- If you have questions about ordering, please call us. You may also fax us at (206) 284-3660 or email us at customer.service@bbks.com.